THE POWER OF FOUR

*Keys to the Hidden Treasures
of the Gospels*

THE
POWER OF FOUR

*Keys to the Hidden Treasures
of the Gospels*

⊕

EDUARDO P. OLAGUER, JR.

Introduction by
Gregory Y. Glazov

 Angelico Press

First published in the USA
by Angelico Press
© Eduardo P. Olaguer, Jr. 2013
Introduction © Gregory Y. Glazov 2013

All scriptural quotations are taken from the
Revised Standard Version, Second Catholic Edition

For information, address:
Angelico Press, 4619 Slayden Rd. NE
Tacoma, WA 98422
www.angelicopress.com

Library of Congress Cataloging-in-Publication
ISBN: 978-1-62138-024-5

Cover Design: Michael Schrauzer
Cover Image: details of mosaics from the
Chapelle des Larmes, Mont Sainte-Odile, Alsace, France

CONTENTS

In memory of my friend
Daewon Byun

Introduction

In *The Power of Four*, Eduardo P. Olaguer, an MIT-trained physical scientist with a keen interest in Scripture, offers several fresh and original insights on the shape of the four Gospels, their relationship to the Old Testament, and their message about Jesus. To introduce his insights, the author observes that Jesus revealed a way of reading the Bible to the disciples at Emmaus, and so endowed them with an understanding of the "big picture." Olaguer then announces his hope to supply the reader with a similar big picture or map of the spiritual journey indicated obscurely by the Scriptures. By means of this introduction, the author clearly shares the belief common to most Jews and Christians that the Scriptures are sealed and require an inspired opening to be understood. The most famous illustration of this belief in the New Testament is precisely St. Luke's account of Jesus' dialogue with the two disciples on the road to Emmaus after his resurrection.

St. Luke relates how Jesus opened the Scriptures to the disciples by explaining what the Law and the Prophets said about him, and how their hearts burned when he did so. Significantly, these disciples did not recognize Jesus then but only later at supper, at his "breaking of bread" with them, at which point he vanished from their sight (Lk 24:25–32). In reflecting on this narrative, I perceive that Jesus did not offer *an* interpretation of the Law and the Prophets, but *the* interpretation. This is to say that while ordinary interpretations of the Scriptures vary in their understanding of its message, Jesus possessed and bestowed a definitive interpretation.

It is important to wonder why the disciples did not recognize Jesus in the opening of the Scriptures but in the breaking of bread. Since "breaking of bread" was a technical term at the time for the celebration of the Eucharist, St. Luke was probably indicating to his audience that henceforth such "breaking of bread" would be the privileged place for experiencing Jesus' presence in the Church. This recognition requires faith and thus depends on a prior grounding in the Scriptures. I conclude that the disciples' recognition of Jesus in the breaking of bread was empowered by his nurturing of their faith through his opening of the Scriptures to them. Consequently, Jesus' opening of the Scriptures flowed into and was completed by the "breaking of bread," so that attempts to reconstruct what he said must wrestle with this linkage.

Initially, Olaguer does not seek to reveal the specific contours of what Jesus said to the disciples at Emmaus, although he later discusses various references to the Eucharist and its precursors in the Old Testament. Rather, Olaguer takes as his principal goal the unlocking of the Four Gospels to explain Jesus' identity and mission. He does this by identifying four types of symbolic patterns or keys, the title, *The Power of Four,* referring to the four keys that unlock the spiritual treasures contained in the Gospels.

The first key is to be discerned in the correlations between the images of Jesus presented by the four Evangelists and the four Cherubim, the latter of which incorporate the forms of man, lion, ox and eagle that make up God's chariot-throne (Ezk 1:10; Rev 4:7). The Fathers of the Church drew this association to highlight that the Evangelists conveyed and enthroned Christ the Word, who inspired and ensouled their Gospels. By this analogy, the Fathers attempted to correlate more precisely the relationship between the four Evangelists and the four Cherubim. Olaguer follows their thinking and sees an important clue to the purpose of the four gospels in communicating and making Christ known. The gospels symbolize earth's four rivers, winds, and corners, as well as the four creatures of the chariot, and thus figuratively encompass the created world. What is new and original in Olaguer's presentation is that, while the Fathers of the Church typically correlate each Evangelist with a single creature, not always agreeing on their identities, Olaguer conflates the ideas of Ambrose, Augustine, and the Apocalypse to propose that Matthew is represented by both the man and the lion, Mark by the lion and the ox, Luke by the ox and the man, and John, who stands alone, by the eagle. This is an interesting and fruitful proposal. Ezekiel in fact says that each creature had four faces (Ezk 1:10), while the Apocalypse may be interpreting each of these faces as a separate creature (Rev 4:6). If this is so, and if the Gospels correspond to the four creatures, Olaguer would have reason to think of them as having more than one face.

The reader who notices the inspiration that Olaguer takes from Jesus' exposition of the Scriptures to the disciples on the road to Emmaus may wonder about the relationship between the first of the four keys and Jesus' discourse. That discourse would have preceded the existence of the written Gospels, and so these could not have been the subject of that conversation. Nonetheless it would have dealt with matters which the author proposes were symbolized by the four creatures: creation and salvation history (man), the election of Israel (lion), the establishment of the Temple and the oracles of the prophets (ox), psalmody and heavenly worship (eagle). Olaguer is thus not attempting a reconstruction of the Emmaus discourse, but offering to explain the shape and character of the Gospels in their developed form.

The second key relates to Israel's Scriptures, the Old Testament, as a coherent whole with Christ as their embodiment. Accordingly, the contents of the Old Testament are essential to the understanding of Christ. This must have been the core of the Emmaus discourse. From that discourse, it would seem that the shape of the Old Testament was at least twofold, including the Law (Moses) and all the Prophets (Lk 24:27). But towards the end of Luke's Gospel we hear of the Law, the Prophets, and the

Psalms, suggesting that the Scriptures were acquiring a third division of Writings, abbreviated in Jewish tradition by the acronym TaNaK (Torah [Law], Nevi'im [Prophets], Ketuvim [Writings]). The Torah consisted of five books of Moses; the Prophets consisted of four books of Former Prophets (Joshua, Judges, Samuel and Kings) and four books of Latter Prophets (Isaiah, Jeremiah, Ezekiel and the Twelve); and the Writings contained the Psalms, Wisdom Books, and other works (including the history of the Chronicler, Ezra, and Nehemiah). In binding the New Testament to the Old, the Church frequently presented the Old in four parts, transferring the Latter Prophets to the end to serve as a bridge between the Old and New Testaments, and gathering historical writings together with the Former Prophets.   Olaguer takes note of the threefold Jewish division but works with the Christian shape of the Bible and the four-fold division of the Old Testament, positing a correspondence between these divisions and the Gospels. Accordingly, he proposes that Matthew corresponds to the Torah, Mark to Joshua and the Nevi'im, Luke to the Historical Books that were counted by the Jews among either the Former Prophets or the Writings, and John to the Wisdom books, including books outside the Jewish canon originally written in Greek (the so-called Deuterocanonicals). Corroboration for this rather original and stimulating proposal comes from the "maps" constituted by the third and fourth keys.

The third key consists of four "maps" correlating the

structure and character of the gospels with their characteristic oratorical devices, identified by the author as *chiasmus* for Matthew, *inclusio* for Mark, *diptych* for Luke, and *parataxis* for John. This proposal resonates with insights common and not so common in New Testament studies. Mark is distinguished by several literary techniques, such as sandwiching of events in the pattern of A-B-A to prompt the reader to meditate on how the middle relates to and interprets the outer to reveal the mystery of Jesus, for example: (A) Jairus pleads with Jesus to save his daughter, (B) Woman with hemorrhage touches Jesus, (A) Jesus raises Jairus' daughter (Mk 5:21–43); or (A) cursing of the fig tree, (B) cleansing of the Temple, (A) withering of the fig tree (Mk 11:12–21). Scholars are intensely interested in Luke's diptychs and there is a trend initiated by the Dominican scholar, Fr. Thomas Brodie, that sees Luke's diptychs structured in groups of eight (the number is significant), beginning with the twofold accounts of annunciation, birth, and visitation, in a spiraling tendency towards greater complexity and volume, and that Luke based this structure on the eightfold Elijah-Elisha narrative, with its ascent/assumption bridge.

The fourth key relates to the variety of ways in which the number seven serves to structure, unify, and emphasize the message of the Gospels, as described in succeeding paragraphs.

Olaguer's chapter on Matthew begins by exploring the linkage between the division of Jesus' genealogy into three series of fourteen generations, and the fourteen lions flanking the throne of Solomon. This introduces Jesus' royal Davidic lineage and presents him as the Lion of Judah. The chapter then seeks to correlate the seven mountains on which Jesus appears (those of the Temptation, Sermon on Mount, Feeding of the Four Thousand, Transfiguration, Olives, Golgotha, Galilee) with seven Mosaic feasts. In the process, the narrative echoes key motifs in the Pentateuch, for example, the Patriarchs in Genesis, the giving of the Law in Exodus, the purity legislation in Leviticus, the rebellions in Numbers, the warning that only children would enter the Promised Land, and the description of Moses completing his preaching and mission beyond the Jordan. These insightful correlations persuade us that Jesus embodies God's creative purpose for humanity and perfects Israel's response to God's revelation as described in the Pentateuch.

St. Mark commences his story of Jesus at the Jordan, which mirrors the events at the beginning of the book of Joshua. Olaguer develops this parallel so that Joshua's conquests, marked by his seven stone memorials at Gilgal, Achor, Ai, Ebal, Makkedah, Jordan, and Shechem, can be seen as delineating the boundaries of spiritual territory conquered by Christ. Parallels with the prophet Elijah suggest that Mark extends the recapitulation of the Former Prophets beyond Joshua into Kings, while Jesus' fulfillment of the Suffering Servant oracles of Isaiah extends this recapitulation even further to include the

Latter Prophets. The Gospel of Mark concisely unpacks the seven points of the original proclamation of the Gospel by St. Peter as presented in Acts, focusing on the Passion of Christ so as to emphasize the victory he gains (lion) through sacrifice (ox). The author's contention that the Gospel of Mark is a rewriting of Joshua and the Nevi'im is interesting and worthy of further study.

In illuminating scholarship, Olaguer demonstrates how St. Luke systematically alludes to the Historical Books of the Old Testament to clarify the mission and identity of Jesus. Luke begins his Gospel in the Temple and weaves his narrative around seven events that take place there: (1) the annunciation of the birth of John the Baptist to Zechariah in the Temple, which echoes the birth of Samuel and his presentation to Eli; (2) the Presentation and (3) Finding of Jesus in the Temple, (4) Christ's Temptation on its Pinnacle, (5) His Cleansing, and (6) Teaching there before the Passion, and (7) the frequenting of the Temple by the Disciples after Jesus' Ascension. The initial diptychs of St. Luke connect John the Baptist/Jesus with Elijah/Elisha and establish a link to the Former Prophets. Luke's emphasis on the Temple also reminds us of the Books of Chronicles counted among the Writings. Jesus in effect recapitulates the seven major events of Israel's history, from just before the founding of Solomon's Temple to its destruction, through the people's exile to Babylon and their restoration, as described in Samuel, Kings and Chronicles.

In mapping the correspondence between the structure of the Gospels and that of the Jewish Scriptures, Olaguer notes that the Gospel of John represents something unique, beginning "anew" and "from above" as it were with allusions to Genesis and the Wisdom books. John's reference to seven signs and seven "I am" sayings to reveal Jesus' person and mission is widely accepted. The author goes further, arguing that in his use of parataxis, John shows that Jesus recapitulates God's works during the seven days of creation. Olaguer includes an excursus which cites respected and established physicists and biologists to propose a "concordist"—as opposed to "creationist"—way of reconciling the biblical account of creation with contemporary science. This approach bypasses, but does not necessarily discount, the parallels between Genesis and Ancient Near Eastern myths of creation, which Catholic biblical scholars generally cite to explain how Genesis prophetically reveals God's word to humanity in language that humans can understand.

How and why Christians rearranged the books in the Hebrew canon is an important question that puzzles many scholars today. It is posited for example that in the Hebrew Bible, the Prophets succeed the Torah to make the Torah applicable to contemporary life, and that the Tanak concludes with the Psalms and the Writings in order to highlight that worship and liturgy represent the goal of the covenant. It is then assumed that Christians divided the Prophets and the Writings so as to create a historical division to succeed the Torah, and placed the Prophets last to present the New Testament as the fulfillment of the Old. If Olaguer's contention that the Four Gospels rewrite the Jewish Scriptures in order to show how Christ is their embodiment, holds true, his insights would also provide a stimulant for the emergence of a fourfold Christian Old Testament canon in the *power of the four* Gospels.

PROF. GREGORY Y. GLAZOV
(SETON HALL UNIVERSITY)

1

Open Book, Closed Treasure

Secret codes behind great works of art or literature are a vulgar cliché. Most of us are familiar with *The Da Vinci Code*, which purports to explain the hidden origins of Christianity as encrypted within the paintings of Leonardo da Vinci and the medieval myth of the Holy Grail. We also have the *Bible Code*, based on the Hebrew Torah, allegedly encapsulating the history and future destiny of the world and every human being. But one "code" that has largely escaped notice by commentators on the Bible is the invisible structure behind the four Gospels of Matthew, Mark, Luke, and John.

A very real thread ties together all the Gospels in a coherent way and also solves the question posed to every reader of the New Testament, namely: Why are there four Gospels? The answer lies in four keys that unlock the deeper meaning of the life of Jesus Christ. Briefly, these keys are as follows:

1) Four allegorical creatures

2) Four sets of Old Testament books

3) Four maps (structural clues)

4) Four treasures of seven symbols

Ancient and modern authorities on the Gospels, from Augustine and Thomas Aquinas to Benjamin Bacon and Raymond Brown, have here and there acknowledged the existence of one or more of these keys, but always in isolation from one another and never with complete reference to all four Gospels. This book brings together in a single place insights on these four keys.

The four keys enable us to perceive the *entire* Bible as the logically systematic work of an Infinite Mind, a view that runs counter to the received wisdom of our age, which perceives Scripture as only a haphazard collection of writings by time and culture-bound human authors. Knowledge of the four keys gives us access to the spiritual treasure of the Gospels by increasing our love and reverence for the Creator. From this awe of God comes faith in his mercy and strength to keep his commandments, for "The fear of the LORD is the beginning of wisdom (Prov 9:10)."

Unlike the Bible Code, which requires a computer to decipher, the code behind the Gospels is hidden in plain view. To discover it, we must dig beneath our prejudices and exchange the fashionable ideas of our day for the fertile field of an open mind. In this way we may fulfill the parable told by Jesus:

> The kingdom of heaven is like a treasure hidden in a field, which a man found and covered up; then in his joy he goes and sells all that he has and buys that field. (Mt 13:44)

You need not spend years of tedious effort to obtain the treasure of the Gospels. Merely turn the pages of this book and heed the invitation given to all by Jesus of Nazareth, who said upon meeting his first disciples, "Come and see (John 1:46)."

2

Deciphering the Gospels

The Way

Reading the Bible can be a daunting task. Slogging through the seemingly endless lists of genealogies, chronologies, laws, ceremonies, proverbs, oracles, wars, and dynastic successions reminds us of that Old Testament prophet and curmudgeon, Isaiah, who said that for many, the word of God would be "precept upon precept, precept upon precept, line upon line, line upon line, here a little, there a little (Is 28:9–10)." In other words, sheer drudgery.

The problem, however, is that we are often stuck with the habit of reading the Bible in linear fashion and, as it were, "in the small." We need to see the big picture, which reveals the Bible to be a series of grand cycles converging towards the man at the heart of its mystery, Jesus Christ.

Luke records that when Jesus rose from the dead after being hung upon the Cross, he appeared to two men, Cleopas and his companion, who were walking the seven miles from Jerusalem to Emmaus. Though the two travelers did not at first recognize Jesus, their hearts burned as they listened to him explain the Jewish Bible in a way they had never heard before. Jesus said to them:

> "O foolish men, and slow of heart to believe all
> that the prophets have spoken!". . . . And begin-
> ning with Moses and all the prophets, he inter-
> preted to them in *all the Scriptures* the things
> concerning himself. (Lk 24:25–27)

What Jesus did for Cleopas and his companion was to
reveal a way of reading the Bible that allowed them to see
the point of it all. He showed them the big picture. In the
same way, we will begin the journey to our own spiritual
Emmaus with a map of where we are going.

The Number of the Gospels

To us, numbers may appear dull and lifeless, but to the
ancient Israelites they possessed spiritual power. The Israelites developed a practice called *gematria*, whereby each
letter of the Hebrew or Greek alphabet was assigned a
numerical value. These values could then be added
together to obtain the equivalent number of an entire
word or phrase, as in the assignment of the infamous
number 666 to the name of the Antichrist (Rev 13:18). A
more benign but lesser known example of *gematria* is
found in Matthew's genealogy of Jesus, whom Matthew
calls "the son of David (Mt 1:1)." As we shall see, Matthew repeatedly uses the number 14, the equivalent of
David's name, in describing the human origins of Christ
(Mt 1:1–17).

A more fundamental application of number mysticism
to the Gospels stems from the Christian concept of God

as three persons: Father, Son, and Holy Spirit. This doctrine of the Trinity is the basis for assigning the number
three to God. The number four then derives its meaning
from the act of creation—God's addition of something
beyond himself by expanding his own unity, represented
by the sum of three plus one. The number four then sym-
bolizes the created world, as in the biblical expressions
"the four rivers [of Eden]," "the four winds," and "the four
corners of the earth."

Christianity differs from Judaism not only in its concept of the Trinity, but also in its doctrine of the Incarnation—the belief that God became man. The Greek word
for "gospel" is *evangelion*, which means "good news." The
Gospel or Good News, which is a continuation of the
word of God in the Old Testament, is that the Second Person of the Trinity, the personification of God's Word,
became man in Jesus Christ to save the human race. In the
Christian scheme of things, there are four Gospels
because they refer to Jesus as the Word of God (John 1:1),
who, according to Genesis, spoke the world into existence ("And God said…"), and who himself came into the
world as the Word Made Flesh (John 1:9–14). In plain
words, the four Gospels speak of God's infinite love for
his creation, expressed by the entering into it of his own.

> For God so loved the world that he gave his only-
> begotten Son, that whoever believes in him
> should not perish but have eternal life. For God

sent the Son into the world, not to condemn the world, but that the world might be saved through him. (John 3:16–17)

The Four Creatures

Because Jesus is the Word of God made flesh, and because the Old Testament is an expression of the Word of God, it is reasonable to suppose that Jesus is somehow an encapsulation or embodiment of the Old Testament. The first chapter in the Book of Ezekiel points to this conclusion. The first ten verses speak of the "word of the Lord" appearing to Ezekiel, enthroned upon four living creatures with four faces and four wings. Each creature had the face of a man in the front, the face of a lion on the right, the face of an ox on the left, and the face of an eagle at the back.

The faces of the four creatures represent four important aspects of the Old Testament fulfilled in Jesus Christ. The first face represents Adam, the first human. The second face recalls the Lion of Judah foreseen by the patriarch Jacob on his deathbed (Gen 49:9). The face of the Lion also recalls the oracle of Balaam concerning Israel on the verge of its conquest of the Promised Land:

Behold, a people! As a lioness it rises up and as a lion it lifts itself; it does not lie down till it devours the prey and drinks the blood of the slain. (Num 23:24)

The third face signifies the animal victims sacrificed in the temple built by King Solomon (2 Ch 7:4), as well as the twelve oxen that plowed Elisha's field until Elisha was recruited by the prophet Elijah (1 Ki 19:19–21). Finally, the fourth face calls attention to the mysterious figure of the Psalms, of whom it is written: "He who dwells in the shelter of the Most High, who abides in the shadow of the Almighty.... He will cover you with his pinions, and under his wings you will find refuge (Ps 91:1–4)."

The four creatures of Ezekiel appear somewhat differently in the last book of the New Testament. In the fourth chapter of the Apocalypse, the throne of God is said to be surrounded by four living creatures: the first like a lion, the second like an ox, the third with the face of a man, and the fourth like a flying eagle. If the four creatures of Ezekiel point to Jesus as the incarnation of the Old Testament, then those of the Apocalypse show him to be the incarnation of the prophetic word. "For the testimony of Jesus is the spirit of prophecy (Rev 19:10)." This is symbolized by the scroll with seven seals opened by the Lamb of God in chapter 5 of the Apocalypse. Jesus therefore embodies all of God's revelation, past, present, and future.

The four creatures of Ezekiel and the Apocalypse have traditionally been employed as symbols of the four Gospels. The Fathers of the Church, however, disagreed as to how these creatures or their faces should be assigned to each Gospel. St. Ambrose assigned the lion to Mark because of the expression of divine power in his Gospel, whereas St. Augustine assigned the lion to Matthew because of the emphasis on Christ's royalty, in his.

Artistic tradition has sided with St. Ambrose in assigning the lion to Mark. One justification for such a match is that the man stands for Matthew, whose Gospel begins with Christ's human genealogy; the lion stands for Mark, whose Gospel begins with John the Baptist crying out like a lion in the desert; the sacrificial ox stands for Luke, whose Gospel begins in the Temple; and the eagle stands for John, whose Gospel begins in heaven with the eternal Word. This particular match corresponds to the order given the faces of the creatures in Ezekiel's vision.

An alternative correspondence is based on the order of the creatures in the Apocalypse. In this schema, Matthew corresponds to the lion because he shows Jesus to be the Lion of Judah, Mark to the ox because he portrays Christ as the Suffering Servant of Isaiah's prophecies (Is 52:13–53:12), Luke to the man because he describes the Nativity of Christ, and John to the eagle because his mystical gospel enables the spirit to soar toward heaven, as described by the prophet Isaiah:

> They who wait for the LORD . . . shall mount up
> with wings like eagles. (Is. 40:31)

As we shall see, both sets of correspondences are essential to understanding the Gospels. Matthew is therefore represented by both man and lion. Mark is both lion and

ox. Luke is both ox and man. And, finally, John is a soar-
ing eagle. As an aside, the Gospel of John is set apart from
the other Gospels in this interpretive scheme, which is
consistent with the significant overlap in material, and
hence in symbolism, found among Matthew, Mark, and
Luke. The correspondence between the four living creatures and the Gospels is the first of the four keys.

The Old Testament

We have already anticipated the second key to the Gospels
by calling Jesus the embodiment of the Old Testament.
Since the days of the early Church, Christians have recognized that the Old and New Testaments form a coherent
whole, as if they had been written by a single author
despite the multitude of centuries, the variety of cultures,
and the different languages that shaped the Bible. For the
Christian, the primary author of Scripture is not man but
the Holy Spirit. This is the foundation of St. Augustine's
teaching that "the New Testament is hidden in the Old,
and the Old Testament is unveiled in the New (*Questions
on the Heptateuch* 2.73)."

To appreciate the connection between the Old and
New Testaments, let us review the various parts of the
Jewish scriptures and the contents thereof. The first five
books of the Old Testament, Genesis, Exodus, Leviticus,
Numbers, and Deuteronomy, are called in Hebrew the
Torah, and in Greek, the Pentateuch or Five Books. They
are also collectively referred to as the Law of Moses,

because a large portion of the Torah consists of various statutes such as the requirement of circumcision, the Ten Commandments, the dietary or *kosher* laws, the rules pertaining to feast days and liturgical celebrations, and many other regulations and proscriptions governing everyday life.

The Book of Joshua, immediately following the Torah, chronicles Israel's conquest of the Promised Land under Joshua's leadership. For the Jews, Joshua is the first book of the collection known in Hebrew as the Nevi'im or Prophets. The Nevi'im were divided into the Former Prophets, consisting of the books of Joshua, Judges, Samuel, and Kings, and the Latter Prophets, consisting of the books of Isaiah, Jeremiah, Ezekiel, and the so-called minor prophets.

Among Christians, the books of Samuel and Kings, together with Chronicles, Ezra, Nehemiah, and Esther, are collectively known as the Historical Books, because they record the history of the people of Israel from the beginning of the monarchy and the construction of the First Temple, until the end of the monarchy, coinciding with the exile of the Jews to Babylon, followed by their return to the Promised Land to build the Second Temple. (In the Catholic Bible, the Historical Books also include the Books of Tobit, Judith, and Maccabees.)

The remainder of the Jewish Bible, outside of the Torah and the Nevi'im, is referred to in Hebrew as the Ketuvim, or Writings. These include what are referred to by

Christians as the Wisdom Books: Job, Psalms, Proverbs, Ecclesiastes, and the Song of Solomon. In the Catholic Bible, these also include the Wisdom of Solomon, and Sirach. To the Ketuvim, the Jews add the books of Ruth, Chronicles, Ezra, Nehemiah, Esther, Lamentations, and Daniel. The combination of the first letters of the Hebrew words, Torah, Nevi'im, and Ketuvim (TNK), accounts for the Jewish name for the Bible, the Tanak.

The Old Testament books are the essential background of the Gospels. The Gospel of Matthew is in fact the Christian equivalent of the Torah, beginning with the stories of the patriarchs in Genesis; the Gospel of Mark, that of Joshua and the Nevi'im; and the Gospel of Luke, that of the Historical Books, some of which are classified among the Former Prophets, while others are considered part of the Ketuvim. The Gospel of John, which was written much later than the other three Gospels, fills in the gaps left by Matthew, Mark, and Luke, mirroring both the Genesis creation story, and the origins of Wisdom as treated in the Old Testament books of the Ketuvim and outside the Tanak. These correspondences form the second key that unlocks the Gospels.

The Maps

The third key consists of four maps that reveal the underlying structures of the four Gospels. Each map is an oratorical device known by a technical term in Greek or Latin.

The map of the Gospel of Matthew is referred to as a *chiasmus*, a rhetorical or literary figure in which words, grammatical constructions, or concepts are repeated in reverse order (e.g., ABCBA), as in a mountain structure where the peak is the center of the chiasmus. The first clue to this structure is the genealogy of Jesus, which takes the form of three series of 14 generations. The first series "ascends" from Abraham to David, whose reign was the peak of the kingdom of Israel. The second "descends" from David to Jechoniah, the king who reigned at the beginning of the Babylonian Exile. Lastly, the third series of 14 generations "re-ascends" from Jechoniah to Christ.

The map of the Gospel of Mark is referred to as an *inclusio*, that is, the use of similar words to begin and end a story or literary segment. The opening eleven verses of the Gospel provide the first example of this structure. The Gospel starts with the words, "The beginning of the gospel of Jesus Christ, the Son of God (Mk 1:1)," and ends with the words of the Father at the baptism of Jesus, "You are my beloved Son, with you I am well pleased (Mk 1:11)."

The map of the Gospel of Luke is referred to as a *diptych*, which is the side-by-side display of related images. The first instance of this structure is the parallel presentation by Luke of the nativities of John the Baptist and Jesus, which contain many similar details including the appearance of the angel Gabriel to announce the conception of both Jesus and his cousin, John.

The key to the Gospel of John is a literary technique known as *parataxis* or the repetitive use of simple words or phrases. The first example is the famous prelude, John 1:1–18, which makes repeated reference to the words, "beginning," "Word," "God," "made," "life," "light," "darkness," "witness," "world," "flesh," "grace," "truth," and "glory." These words and several others constitute the "atomic elements" of John's Gospel.

The Seven-fold Treasures

The fourth key to the Gospels is based on the mystical number seven. If the number four represents the created world, then the sum of four and three epitomizes the union of God with creation. God became man in Jesus Christ to pursue a bride, the Church. Through his union with this bride, a new creation will be brought forth in which all things mirror the glory of God without blemish. This mystical union, symbolized by the New Jerusalem of the Apocalypse (Rev 21:1–5), is the ultimate goal of the Incarnation. Pointing the way to the New Jerusalem is a seven-fold treasure of symbols within each of the four Gospels.

The seven-fold treasure of the Gospel of Matthew consists of seven mountains upon which the seven priorities of the Gospel are set forth. These priorities correspond to the seven feasts ordained by Moses in the Torah.

The seven-fold treasure of the Gospel of Mark consists of seven remembrances that were the original proclamation of the gospel by St. Peter, one of many early evangelical proclamations that scholars refer to in summary using the technical term, *kerygma* or proclamation. These remembrances correspond to the seven stone memorials built by the Israelites during their conquest of the Promised Land, from the crossing of the Jordan at Gilgal to the final covenant between Joshua and Israel at Shechem.

The seven-fold treasure of the Gospel of Luke consists of seven visits to the Temple of Jerusalem, corresponding to seven major events in the history of Israel, from the time of the judge Samuel to the end of the Babylonian Exile. The seven temple visits of Luke's Gospel mark the road that leads to spiritual growth in Jesus Christ.

The seven-fold treasure of the Gospel of John consists of seven signs revealing the true identity of Jesus Christ as God's Wisdom and the bearer of his mysterious name, I AM. They remind us of the original seven days of creation, and foreshadow the new creation of which Jesus is the new beginning.

In the remainder of this work, we will explore the four Gospels in greater detail according to the four keys, corresponding to the four sections in each of the four subsequent chapters.

3

The New Moses:
The Gospel of Matthew

The Man and the Lion

Solomon, the brilliant son and successor of King David, identified in *gematria* by the number fourteen, possessed a marvelous throne of gold and ivory (2 Ch 9:17–19). His throne was flanked by two lions and had six steps leading to it, each of which was also flanked by two lions. King Solomon and the fourteen lions guarding his throne help explain why St. Matthew's Gospel begins with a genealogy, summarized by the declaration that Jesus Christ is "the son of David, the son of Abraham (Mt 1:1)."

To Abraham God had pledged, "I will make nations of you, and kings shall come forth from you (Gen 17:6)," while to David he promised, "I will raise up your offspring after you, who shall come forth from your body . . . and I will establish the throne of his kingdom forever (2 Sam 7:12–13)." The covenants with David and Abraham had in common two divine guarantees: (1) an enduring line of descent, and (2) royalty and kingship (Gen 17:1–14; 2 Sam 7:1–29, 23:5). The image of the man traditionally assigned to the Gospel of Matthew represents the fruit of the first promise, while that of the lion the fulfillment of the second.

Genealogies occupy a prominent place in the Bible because they establish the truth of God's covenant. Matthew's genealogy of Jesus is particularly important because his Gospel was addressed to the Jews, who, as monotheists, and in contrast to the Greeks and Romans, had difficulty accepting Jesus' divine origin. By emphasizing his human descent from David and Abraham, Matthew presents Jesus as the Son of the Covenant, the embodiment of all the Jews held dear, most especially the covenant of Mount Sinai (Ex 19:1–6, 24:1–18). It was at Sinai that God swore to Israel, You shall be my own possession among all peoples [the people of the Man]...and you shall be to me a kingdom of priests and a holy nation [the kingdom of the Lion] (Ex 19:5–6)."

The kingdom that God promised Israel was ultimately a spiritual one, whose mysterious nature Jesus explained to his disciples through parables, saying, "To you it has been given to know the secrets of the kingdom of heaven (Mt 13:11)." Like the golden Ark hidden behind the veil of the Tabernacle (Ex 26:33), the kingdom of God rests within the soul of man as the secret at the heart of the Divine Covenant. This covenant was fulfilled by the man Jesus, the Lion of Judah, who taught us to pray always to our Father in heaven, "Thy kingdom come (Mt 6:10)."

The New Torah

The Torah is derived from the book that Moses read on Mount Sinai on the day he ratified the Old Covenant by sprinkling the blood of a bull on an altar (Ex 24:7). The Gospel of Matthew was intended by God to be the New Torah, the Book of the New Covenant ratified by the blood of Jesus on Calvary. All five books of the Torah are represented in Matthew's gospel according to their traditional order: Genesis (Mt 1:1–2:15), Exodus (Mt 2:16–7:29), Leviticus (Mt 8:1–11:1), Numbers (Mt 11:2–18:35), and Deuteronomy (Mt 19:1–28:20). These sections are in most cases separated by the formula, "when Jesus finished these words," or by a similar phrase (Mt 7:28, 11:1, 19:1).

Matthew 1:1 begins directly with the "book" of the generations or "genesis" (in Greek, *biblos geneseos*) of Jesus, recalling the verse in Genesis, "This is the book of the generations of Adam (Gen 5:1)." Jesus' legal father, St. Joseph, was named after the favorite son of the patriarch Israel, also known as Jacob. Joseph, the son of Israel, was sold into slavery by his eleven brothers, but eventually rose to the highest office in Egypt. He then married the daughter of the priest of On (Gen 41:45) and served as "a father to Pharaoh (Gen 45:8)." Similarly, St. Joseph was the head of the Holy Family, the spouse of the Virgin Mary, and the foster father of Jesus. Like his counterpart in Genesis, St. Joseph received messages from God in dreams and brought his family to Egypt in response to a crisis.

The crisis which took the Holy Family to Egypt was King Herod's slaughter of the Innocents (Mt 2:16–18). This event mirrors the transition from Genesis to Exodus in the Torah, and Pharaoh's massacre of the infant sons of the Hebrews, from which Moses had been delivered (Ex 1:15–2:10). Jesus, Mary, and Joseph would eventually return from Egypt to Galilee after the death of Herod, enabling Matthew to quote the prophet Hosea: "Out of Egypt I called my son (Hos 11:1, Mt 2:15)."

The parallel between Matthew and Exodus reaches its peak in the Sermon on the Mount in which Jesus established the Law of the New Covenant, just as God gave Moses the Ten Commandments. To inaugurate the kingdom of God, Jesus first had to be baptized in the Jordan and undergo temptation in the desert for forty days. Only then did he proceed to the mountain in Galilee where he began his Sermon by announcing the Beatitudes (blessings). This sequence of events recounted by Matthew mirrors Israel's journey through the Red Sea, the wandering in the desert of Sinai for forty years, and the passage between the mountains Gerizim and Ebal, where both blessings and curses were pronounced on the Israelites, according to their degree of obedience to the Law of Moses (De 27:11–28:14). The curses of the Law correspond to Jesus' condemnation of the scribes and Pharisees in Mt 23, part of the section paralleling Deuteronomy.

The Book of Leviticus, which follows Exodus in the Torah, describes various purification ceremonies for leprosy and other forms of ritual uncleanness. The corresponding section in Matthew begins with Jesus' healing of a leper and his command to "show yourself to the priest and offer the gift Moses prescribed (Mt 8:4)." Matthew then compares Jesus to the scapegoat that bore the sins of the Israelites away from their camps (Lev 16:20–28), quoting the prophet Isaiah, "He took away our infirmities and bore our diseases (Is 53:4; Mt 8:17)." These infirmities and diseases are both physical and spiritual. When Jesus called Matthew to be his disciple, the Jews objected to his choice because Matthew, also known as Levi, was a tax collector. Jesus replied, "Those who are well do not need a physician, but the sick do.... I did not come to call the righteous but sinners (Mt 9:12)."

Besides ritual purity, the law of Leviticus also governed the ordination and conduct of priests (the descendants of Israel's son, Levi), forbidding them to touch a dead person. In the case of the high priest, "not even for his father and mother may he thus be unclean or leave the sanctuary (Lev 21:12)." Jesus insisted on the same high standard in recruiting his own disciples. When one of his followers said to him, "Lord, let me go first and bury my father (Mt 8:21)," he replied, "Let the dead bury their dead (Mt 8:22)."

Jesus' healing ministry increasingly antagonized the leaders of the Jewish religion. Matthew recounts the heightened opposition to Jesus by the scribes, Pharisees, and Sadducees, recalling the rebellion against Moses led by Korah, Dathan, and Abiram (Num 16:1–35). Jesus called the Pharisees and Sadducees "blind guides (Mt 15:14)," suggesting a comparison with the flawed prophet Balaam, who was blinded to the appearance of an angel by his greed for gold and silver (Num 22:1–35).

The stories of the rebellion of Korah, Dathan, and Abiram, and of Israel's encounter with the prophet Balaam, both appear in the Book of Numbers. Numbers is named after two censuses conducted by Moses at the beginning and towards the end of the forty year exodus (Num 1:1–54, 26:1–65). According to the Book of Numbers, God punished his people for their faithlessness by allowing only the children of those who were counted in the first census to enter the Promised Land (Num 14:22–31). With the exceptions of Joshua and Caleb, it was these children who were counted in the second census before Joshua led Israel across the Jordan, a lesson passed on to us by the popular song, "When the Saints Come Marching In." Likewise, Jesus warns us in St. Matthew's Gospel, "Amen, I say to you, unless you turn and become like children, you will not enter the kingdom of heaven (Mt 18:3)."

Matthew's final section begins with the sentence, "When Jesus finished these words, he left Galilee and went to the district of Judaea across the Jordan (Mt 19:1)." By divine coincidence, Deuteronomy opens with the phrase, "These are the words which Moses spoke to all

Israel beyond the Jordan (De 1:1)." As Moses recapitu-
lated the Law before ascending to his death on Mount
Nebo, Jesus summarized the New Law (Mt 22:34–40)
before his crucifixion on Calvary. Moses' entombed body
would never be found by the Israelites (De 34:6), and neither would the Jews find the risen body of Jesus. Only to
his own disciples did the risen Christ appear at the final
mountain in Galilee (Mt 28:11–20).

Up and Down

Several commentators have noted Matthew's fondness for
the rhetorical pattern known as *chiasmus*, as discussed earlier in the case of Jesus' genealogy. *The Expositor's Bible
Commentary* identifies David Wenham as the first modern
scholar to notice the chiastic arrangement of the Parables
in Mt 13. The commentators John Fenton and Thomas
Constable have posited that Matthew's entire Gospel is a
chiasmus centered on Jesus' exposition of the kingdom of
God through the parables. It is no accident then that
mountains are prominently featured in Matthew, for the
up-and-down movement centered on the mountain peak
is a physical representation of the chiasmus.

The *chiasmus* or mountain structure of the Gospel of St.
Matthew is an important clue to Matthew's ultimate message. It recalls the question posed by Moses regarding the
Law: "Now what I am commanding you today is not too
difficult for you or beyond your reach. It is not up in

heaven, so that you have to ask, 'Who will ascend into heaven to get it and proclaim it to us so that we may obey it?' (De 30:11–12)"

Matthew teaches us that we ascend not solely by our own efforts to reach God and keep his commandments. Rather, God's Word himself descended from heaven to give us the power to keep the Law through faith. St. Paul conveyed this very teaching in his Epistle to the Romans:

> Moses describes in this way the righteousness that is by the law: "The man who does these things will live by them." But the righteousness that is by faith says: "Do not say in your heart, 'Who will ascend into heaven?'" (that is, to bring Christ down) "or 'Who will descend into the deep?'" (that is, to bring Christ up from the dead). But what does it say? "The word is near you; it is in your mouth and in your heart," that is, the word of faith we are proclaiming: That if you confess with your mouth, "Jesus is Lord," and believe in your heart that God raised him from the dead, you will be saved. (Rom 10:5–9)

The trusting acceptance of Christ's divine actions on our behalf is a sure remedy for sin that does not depend on the collective moral success (the upward slopes) or failure (the downward slopes) of the human race. Jesus' incarnation and death, by which he descended from heaven to earth and then from earth to the netherworld, and his resurrection from the dead that preceded his ascension into heaven, mysteriously save us from the condemnation of the Law.

The Seven Mountains

When God made a covenant with Abraham, he identified himself as *El Shaddai* (Gen 17:1–2), meaning "God of the mountains." Similarly the prophet Isaiah announced, "How beautiful upon the mountains are the feet of him who brings good tidings (Is 52:7)." The good news of Matthew is outlined by Jesus' actions that took place on seven mountains, corresponding to the seven feasts established by Moses in the Torah (Lev 23:1–44).

The Temptation in the Desert: Jesus overcame Satan (*Mt 4:1–11*)

During the Exodus, Moses won a battle against the Amalekites while standing on a mountain in the wilderness of Rephidim (Ex 17:8–16). Jesus likewise overcame the temptation of Satan on a desert mountain (Mt 4:8), succeeding at the very challenges that the Israelites had failed as they crossed the desert of Sinai.

Whereas the Israelites had lost faith in Divine Providence and grumbled at the lack of food (Ex 16:1–15), Jesus refused to relieve his hunger from fasting by turning stones into bread. He quoted Deuteronomy, "Man shall not live by bread alone, but by every word that proceeds from the mouth of God (De 8:5, Mt 4:4)."

The Israelites had doubted that God was among them; they put him to the test when they pined for water at Massah and Meribah (Ex 17:1–7, De 6:16, Ps 95:8–9). Jesus, on the contrary, maintained true hope in God. He refused to presume upon God's protection by throwing himself off the temple parapet, as Satan suggested. Again he quoted Deuteronomy, "You shall not put the LORD, your God, to the test (De 6:16, Mt 4:7)."

The Israelites had violated the love of God when they worshipped the golden calf (Ex 32:1–20), unlike Jesus who refused to worship Satan in exchange for all the kingdoms of the world. Yet again, Jesus quoted Deuteronomy, "You shall worship the LORD your God and him only shall you serve (De 6:13, Mt 4:10)."

Jesus is the only begotten Son of God, who was also the first born into God's kingdom on earth through baptism. The first mountain of Matthew's Gospel reminds us that Jesus lived a perfect life despite the temptation of the devil. Uniting ourselves with Christ in baptism enables us to satisfy the Law through the virtues of faith, hope, and love (1 Cor 13:13), the chief fruits of the Christian life. Jesus' victory over sin, temptation, and the devil immediately after his baptism in the Jordan is symbolized by the Feast of First Fruits (*Bikkurim*), in which the Israelites consecrated the first sheaves of the barley harvest to God (Lev 23:9–14).

The Sermon on the Mount:
Jesus conveys the Spirit of the Law
(Mt 5:1–7:2)

Jesus established the New Covenant as a counterpart to
the Old Covenant of Sinai. In the Old Covenant, the Law
was external to human beings and could never be kept per-
fectly, as amply demonstrated by the history of Israel. In
the New Covenant, the commandments are inscribed by
grace on the hearts of those who trust God, as foretold by
Jeremiah.

> Behold, the days are coming, says the LORD,
> when I will make a new covenant with the house
> of Israel and the house of Judah, not like the cove-
> nant which I made with their fathers when I took
> them by the hand to bring them out of the land of
> Egypt, my covenant which they broke, though I
> was their husband, says the LORD. But this is the
> covenant which I will make with the house of
> Israel after those days, says the LORD: I will put
> my law within them, and I will write it upon their
> hearts; and I will be their God, and they shall be
> my people. (Jer 31:31–33)

The Torah itself foretold the New Covenant. In Exodus,
the Ten Commandments and other aspects of the Law of
Moses are given twice: first as the original tablets of the
Law, engraved by God and given to Moses and the second
after Moses smashed the first tablets in anger upon dis-

covering the golden calf. Moses then wrote with his own finger a second set of tablets to replace the first. The original tablets of the Law represent the Old Covenant and the Israelites' hearts of stone that failed to keep even the first of the Ten Commandments. The second set, written by Moses with his own finger, foreshadowed the New Covenant in which the Holy Spirit would write the Law directly upon the human heart (2 Cor 3:3).

Jesus did not come to abolish the Law but to fulfill it (Mt 5:17). Many ritual aspects of the Law were fulfilled once and for all by Christ's sacrifice of himself on the Cross, to which the Law pointed. Those aspects of the Law that remain as universal requirements, such as the Ten Commandments, the proscriptions of marriage of close kin, and the prohibitions of various forms of sexual misconduct, are properly fulfilled only in union with Christ. In fact, Jesus went beyond the literal law in demanding a far more rigorous form of righteousness, one that unambiguously prohibited divorce and regarded even a stealthy glance as the sin of adultery. No one can adhere to this supreme standard of conduct, except by the grace of God and the power of the Holy Spirit.

It was on the Jewish feast of Pentecost (*Shavuot*), celebrating the first fruit of the wheat harvest, that the Holy Spirit descended upon Jesus' disciples (Acts 2:1–3). Those who accepted the gospel on that day would have the Law of the New Covenant written on their hearts. They were the first fruit of the human harvest that would form the bread of Christ's mystical body (the Church), foreshadowed by the grain and loaves offered to God on each Pentecost (Lev 23:16–20).

The Feeding of the Four Thousand:
Jesus nourishes us
(Mt 15:29–38)

The image of bread as a metaphor for Divine Providence is universally accepted among Jews and Christians. During the Exodus, when Israel had to travel for many years across the barren desert, God fed his people the heavenly bread they called "manna." This miracle has its counterpart in Matthew's Gospel, in which Jesus twice multiplied loaves and fish to feed crowds of five thousand (Mt 14:13–21) and four thousand (Mt 15:29–38).

Food had an important place in the Old Covenant. Many are familiar with the Jewish distinction between clean (*kosher*) and unclean food (Lev 11:1–47), and know that because of this, practicing Jews do not eat pork or shellfish. Jesus, however, wished his disciples to see beyond the external aspect of this law, saying, "Do you not see that whatever goes into the mouth passes into the stomach, and so passes on? But whatever comes out of the mouth proceeds from the heart, and this defiles a man (Mt 15:17–18)."

The Jews' abstention from unclean food was accompanied by their avoidance of contact with the Gentiles, who remained outside the Covenant. When Jesus traveled through the Gentile districts of Tyre and Sidon, he was besieged by a woman begging him to heal her daughter possessed by a demon (Mt 15:21–28). Though Jesus reminded her that "it is not fair to take the children's bread and throw it to the dogs (Mt 15:26)," she replied, "Yes, Lord, yet even the dogs eat the crumbs that fall from their master's table (Mt 25:27)." Her faith pleased Jesus, who then healed her daughter in an instant.

Jesus' mercy on the Gentile woman and her daughter shows us the true gift that lies beneath every blessing we receive from God. When Jesus performed the second of his two miracles of feeding, he stood on a mountain (Mt 15:29) gazing at the people who had come to him for healing and said, "I have compassion on the crowd, because they have been with me now three days, and have nothing to eat (Mt 15:32)."

It is the merciful and compassionate love of God called "grace" that is the real food for our souls. The true object of the Law is to allow God's love to feed us, and others through us, rather than to enable us to feed ourselves. The Pharisees and Sadducees had failed to recognize this in their teachings, substituting for it the pursuit of self-righteousness. It is because of this that Jesus warned his disciples when they had forgotten to bring any bread (Mt 16:5), "Take heed and beware of the leaven of the Pharisees and Sadducees (Mt 16:6)."

During the Feast of Unleavened Bread (*Hag Hamatzah*) that accompanied the Passover (Ex 12:14–20, Lev 23:6–

8), the Israelites had to search diligently for and remove any leaven in their homes and eat only unleavened bread for seven days. Jesus' miracles of the loaves and fish remind us that we are to feed only on the love of God, and avoid the leaven of sin that defiles us and makes us unfit to keep his commandments.

The Transfiguration:
Jesus fulfills the Law and the Prophets
(Mt 17:1–13)

The great mountain to which Moses led the Israelites after crossing the Red Sea was the occasion of a theophany, that is, a visible manifestation of God. This theophany took place immediately after Moses sprinkled the blood of a bull on the altar of sacrifice he had built on Mount Sinai, saying "Behold the blood of the covenant which the LORD has made with you (Ex 24:8)."

> Then Moses and Aaron, Nadab, and Abihu, and seventy of the elders of Israel went up, and they saw the God of Israel; and there was under his feet as it were a pavement of sapphire stone, like the very heaven for clearness. And he did not lay his hand on the chief men of the people of Israel; they beheld God, and ate and drank. . . . Then Moses went up on the mountain, and the cloud covered the mountain. The glory of the LORD settled on Mount Sinai, and the cloud covered it six

days; and on the seventh day he called to Moses
out of the midst of the cloud (Ex 24:9–16).

In Matthew's Gospel, the event corresponding to this
theophany is the Transfiguration, which according to
Christian tradition took place on Mount Tabor. After Jesus
had miraculously fed the crowd of four thousand, he dis-
missed the crowd and traveled by boat to the region of
Magadan (Mt 15:29), where he began to tell the disciples
of his coming passion and death in Jerusalem (Mt 16:21).

> And after six days Jesus took with him Peter and
> James and John his brother, and led them up a
> high mountain apart. And he was transfigured
> before them, and his face shone like the sun, and
> his garments became white as light. And behold,
> there appeared to them Moses and Elijah, talking
> with him. And Peter said to Jesus, "Lord, it is well
> that we are here; if you wish, I will make three
> booths here, one for you and one for Moses and
> one for Elijah." He was still speaking, when lo, a
> bright cloud overshadowed them, and a voice
> from the cloud said, "This is my beloved Son,
> with whom I am well pleased; listen to him." (Mt
> 17:1–5)

Note the parallels between Matthew and the Torah,
including the six days preceding the voice from the cloud.
The appearance of Elijah together with Moses is another
significant detail, since Elijah had also fled from persecu-

tion to Mount Sinai (also known as Horeb), and was fed miraculously along the way (1 Ki 19:4–9). Once he reached the mountain, Elijah spoke to God, as did Moses, and as they both would to Jesus on Mount Tabor.

Jesus is the fulfillment of the Law and the Prophets, represented by Moses and Elijah, who were witnesses of the Old Covenant. It was during *Pesach*, the Feast of Passover (Ex 12:1–13), that Jesus would eat and drink with his disciples, as Moses and the elders of Israel ate and drank in the company of God without fear of death. The blood of the Covenant protected the elders as had the blood of the Passover Lamb that the Israelites sprinkled on the lintels and doorposts of their houses in Egypt (Ex 12:7).

Matthew's presentation of Jesus as the true Passover Lamb was later made explicit by John, who referred to Jesus as "the Lamb of God who takes away the sin of the world (John 1:29)." At the Last Supper, Jesus reminded his disciples of what he had told them at Mount Tabor (Mt 17:12).

> Now as they were eating, Jesus took bread, and blessed, and broke it, and gave it to the disciples and said, "Take, eat; this is my body. And he took a cup, and when he had given thanks he gave it to them, saying, "Drink of it, all of you; for this is my blood of the covenant, which is poured out for many for the forgiveness of sins". (Mt 26:26–28)

42

In the liturgical Christian churches, including the Catholic, Orthodox, Lutheran, and Anglican traditions, the Lord's Supper (also known as the Eucharist) is not merely a commemorative meal, but a theophany akin to the Transfiguration. Mount Tabor represents the summit of Christian faith, as it points to Jesus and his Eucharistic manifestation as the proper focus of divine worship.

The Mount of Olives:
Jesus will return to judge humanity
(Mt 24:1–25:46)

The Mount of Olives is a ridge in eastern Jerusalem that for over 1,000 years before Jesus had been in use as a cemetery by the Jews. It was a fitting place for Jesus' discourse on the Last Judgment. As he sat on the mount, Jesus enumerated the signs that will accompany his return at the end of the world to judge both the spiritually living and the spiritually dead. He ended his discourse with the famous parable of the sheep and the goats, in which he says to the sheep of all nations, "Come, O blessed of my Father, inherit the kingdom prepared for you from the foundation of the world (Mt 25:34)."

Among the seven feasts established by Moses in the Torah was the Feast of Tabernacles, known as *Sukkoth* in Hebrew. During the feast, the Jews made a pilgrimage to Jerusalem and lived for seven days in makeshift booths constructed from palm fronds, leaves, and the boughs of trees. *Sukkoth* was also referred to as the Feast of Ingathering (Ex 23:16), referring to the harvest at the end of the year. Jesus' discourse on the Mount of Olives is fittingly represented by *Sukkoth*, as his Second Coming will be the final harvest of the human race, during which the blessed of all nations will dwell in the heavenly Jerusalem for all eternity.

Golgotha:
Jesus died to atone for our sins
(Mt 27:33–56)

Calvary is a translation of the Latin equivalent of Golgotha, which in turn comes from an Aramaic phrase meaning Place of the Skull (Mt 27:33). Golgotha may also be derived from *Gol Goatha*, meaning Mount of Execution, consistent with the Christian tradition that Jesus was crucified on a hill overlooking the city of Jerusalem.

It was on Golgotha that Jesus died in atonement for all the sins of the human race, fulfilling the meaning behind the animal sacrifices instituted by Moses in the Torah. The greatest of these sacrifices took place on the feast known as *Yom Kippur*, translated as Day of Atonement because of its description in Leviticus.

> And it shall be a statute to you forever that in the seventh month, on the tenth day of the month, you shall afflict yourselves, and shall do no work . . . for on this day shall atonement be made for you, to cleanse you; from all your sins you shall be clean before the LORD. (Lev 16:29–30)

Atonement for the sins of Israel was made once a year on *Yom Kippur* by the high priest, who would pass through the veil of the Holy of Holies of the Tabernacle to sprinkle the blood of a bull on the mercy seat of the Ark of the Covenant (Lev 16:12–16). Jesus' death on the hill of Golgotha is the ultimate sacrifice that opens the door to a relationship with God, for at the moment he died, "the curtain of the temple was torn in two, from top to bottom (Mt 27:51)."

The Mountain of Galilee:
Jesus sends us to announce the gospel
(*Mt* 28:16–20)

Matthew ends with the commissioning of the disciples on a mountain in Galilee. It was there that the resurrected Christ instructed them to evangelize the nations of the world, "teaching them to observe all that I have commanded you (Mt 28:20)." The gospel echoes from this last of the seven mountains like the trumpet blasts that marked *Rosh Hashanah*, the Feast of Trumpets (Lev 23:24). The New Law based on the grace of God has in this way been passed down to us through the centuries, for Jesus, the New Moses, promised his disciples, "I am with you always to the close of the age (Mt 28:20)."

4

The New Joshua:
The Gospel of Mark

The Lion and the Ox

According to tradition, Mark's Gospel was written in Rome where Mark served as secretary to St. Peter, one of the two apostolic founders of the Roman Church (the other being St. Paul). Peter and Mark preached to a Gentile audience familiar with Greco-Roman mythology, which glorified superheroes like Hercules and Perseus, the human sons of the chief god, Zeus or Jupiter. This cultural preparation made it easier for the Romans to accept that Jesus was "the Son of God (Mk 1:1)," as declared by Mark at the beginning of his gospel.

Mark's famous symbol is the Lion. Whereas the Jews regarded this symbol as an icon of royalty and the Davidic dynasty, the Romans would have appreciated it more as an expression of power, as did St. Ambrose of Milan. The Roman Empire, after all, was built on conquest and the victories of its legions, and indeed Mark presents Jesus as a divine conqueror. The defeated demons he cast out from a man into a herd of swine were compelled to tell him, "My name is Legion; for we are many (Mk 5:9)." All Hell quivered before Jesus, just as the unclean spirit in the synagogue cried out to him, "What have you to do with us, Jesus of Nazareth? Have you come to destroy us? (Mk 1:24)"

Jesus' victories spanned the entire creation. He overcame nature by calming a storm on the Sea of Galilee (Mk 4:35–41), by walking on water (Mk 6:45–51), and by withering an unfruitful fig tree (Mk 11:12–21). He conquered disease by healing a leper (Mk 1:40–45), a paralytic (Mk 2:1–12), a man with a withered hand (Mk 3:1–6), a deaf and dumb man (Mk 7:31–37), and the blind Bartimaeus (Mk 10:46–52). Death itself was no match for Jesus, as he raised Jairus' little daughter even as her mourners were wailing in despair (Mk 5:35–43). Jesus' ultimate victories, however, were in the world of the spirit, which he mastered through his own death and resurrection.

Although Mark's emphasis on Jesus' power and authority would have appealed to the Roman nobility, the early Roman church was probably made up mostly of commoners, many of them slaves from other parts of the empire. Latin may have been the native tongue of Rome, but it was not the *lingua franca* of its diverse subjects. That place belonged to Koine Greek, which had been the common tongue, particularly in the East, since the conquests of Alexander the Great.

Whereas Papias, the disciple of John the Evangelist, indicates that Matthew may have originally written his

Gospel in Hebrew or Aramaic, Mark chose to write his in a very unliterary Koine Greek. Exceptions to this were Jesus' words in Aramaic: "*Talitha cumi* (Mk 5:41)," which he spoke in raising the daughter of Jairus, and his cry of abandonment, "*Eloi, Eloi, lama sabachthani?* (Mk 15:34)." Mark's choice of language and humble style reflected his audience of ordinary citizens. For them, the hard working ox may have been a symbol for Christ on par with the lion. Mark indeed depicted Jesus as a tireless servant, using the Greek word *euthys* ("immediately") over fifty times to describe the breathless pace at which Christ went about doing good.

Roman converts to Christianity were initially tolerated by the Empire in deference to Judaism, Christianity being regarded as one of its many sects. Eventually, however, these converts would be severely persecuted by the emperor Nero, who had St. Peter crucified on Vatican Hill, probably around the time that Mark wrote his Gospel. Under these conditions, the Roman Christians would have appreciated the symbol of the ox even more, for the sacrificial ox stood for Christ as the Suffering Servant of the Book of Isaiah, by whose bitter stripes we are healed (Is 53:4-5).

Mark is the shortest of the four Gospels, because it focuses less on Jesus' teachings and more on the Passion of Christ, who "came not to be served, but to serve, and to give his life as a ransom for many (Mk 10:44-45)." In this the Roman martyrs imitated Jesus. Their blood, together with the blood of Jesus, would be the seed of the Church. Rome itself would turn out to be the new promised land conquered by "the gospel of Jesus Christ, the Son of God (Mk 1:1)," the victorious Lion, the blood-stained Ox.

Crossing the Jordan

Jesus was named after Joshua, the successor of Moses who led Israel across the Jordan. It is no coincidence that Mark's Gospel, the New Testament equivalent of the Book of Joshua, begins at the Jordan River, with Jesus' baptism by his cousin John.

The baptism that initiated Jesus' public ministry mirrored Joshua's circumcision of the Israelites—that is, the tearing of their foreskins at Gilgal after they crossed the Jordan (Jos 5:2–9). Mark is the only evangelist who describes the heavens as being "torn" as Jesus came out of the water (Mk 1:10), when the Holy Spirit descended upon him in answer to Isaiah's ancient prayer, "O that you would tear the heavens and come down (Is 64:1)."

The significance of Jesus' baptism is reinforced by Mark's description of John the Baptist, who evoked memories of Elijah the prophet (Mk 1:4–6, 2 Ki 1:8). Elijah had ascended to heaven from the bank of the Jordan opposite Jericho, after which his successor Elisha tore Elijah's cloak in two, then parted the waters in crossing over to the other side (2 Ki 2:13–15). It was there, and in the same miraculous manner, that Joshua had led Israel across the Jordan to Gilgal and Jericho (Jos 4:19). If recent archeological discoveries are to be believed, it was precisely there also that John baptized Jesus.

Joshua and Elijah, to whom Jesus and John correspond, were considered by the Jews to be among the Former Prophets of Israel. Isaiah, on the other hand, was counted among the Latter Prophets. Mark's Gospel thus complements Matthew's evocation of the Torah by presenting Jesus as the fulfillment of the Nevi'im, beginning with Joshua, who, like the prophets that followed, urged fidelity to the Covenant of Sinai as a condition for Israel to maintain the inheritance they gained from God by crossing the Jordan.

End to End

Joshua conquered the Promised Land from one end to the other, starting with the southern portion from Jericho to Gaza (Jos 10), and then north of Gilgal all the way to Hazor above the Sea of Galilee (Jos 11). His military strategy employs a sort of "sandwich" enclosing the entire land in the grip of the Israelites.

Mark's Gospel also employs a sandwich technique. On a small scale, this is known as *inclusio*, which, as noted earlier, means the use of the same or similar words to start and end a story. On a larger scale, the technique is referred to as "intercalation," wherein one story becomes the filling in the sandwich of another story, such as the healing of the woman with a flow of blood sandwiched within the story of Jairus' daughter (Mk 5:22–43).

The two major inclusions of Mark's Gospel link Jesus' baptism to his transfiguration (Mk 9:2–13) and to his death on the Cross (Mk 15:33–39). They are indicated by references to Jesus as God's Son and to the prophet Elijah, as well as by the occurrence of some or all of the words: "torn," "spirit" or "breath" (identical words in Greek and Hebrew), and "voice" or "cry." We also see a significant *inclusio* in the references to Jesus' shining white garments at the Transfiguration (Mk 9:3), and to the young man dressed in a white robe at Jesus' tomb on the day of his resurrection (Mk 16:5).

Mark's use of this literary technique highlights the central mysteries of Christ's Baptism, Transfiguration, Death, and Resurrection. These mysteries are subtly alluded to in the parable of the growing seed (Mk 4:26–29) unique to Mark's gospel. Christ's baptism rains the water of the Holy Spirit upon the seed of God's kingdom, tearing it open to produce the blade. The blade is nurtured by the soil of Scripture, the Law and the Prophets symbolized by the Transfiguration. It is lifted up in the stalk of the Cross that bears the ear of Christ's resurrected body. The ear then produces fruit in the Church and its members, who will be harvested at the Last Judgment.

Mark's inclusions effectively divide his Gospel into two roughly equal portions: (1) from the Baptism of Jesus to the Transfiguration (Mk 1:1–9:1), and (2) from the Transfiguration to the Death and Resurrection of Christ (Mk 9:2–16:20). The first half of the Gospel progressively unveils the mystery of Jesus as the promised Messiah (Christ or "Anointed One"), the fulfillment of Daniel's prophecy concerning "an anointed one [who] shall be cut off (Dan 9:26)." Jesus first kept this identity a secret, warning others not to speak of his miracles (e.g., Mk 1:43–44). Only after Peter recognized him as the Christ (Mk 8:29) did Jesus begin to reveal his destiny of suffering (Mk 8:31). In the second half of Mark's Gospel, Jesus repeatedly draws attention to this prophecy (Mk 9:12, 9:31, 10:33–34, 10:45, 12:7) until the climax of his Passion in Jerusalem.

In the end, "the Lord Jesus . . . was taken up into heaven, and sat down at the right hand of God (Mk 16:19)."

> [God] raised him from the dead and made him sit at his right hand in the heavenly places, far above all rule and authority and power and dominion, and above every name that is named, not only in this age but also in that which is to come, and he has put all things under his feet and has made him head over all things for the Church, which is his body, the fullness of him who fills all in all. (Eph 1:20–23)

> Then comes the end, when he delivers the kingdom to God the Father after destroying every rule and every authority and power. For he must reign until he has put all his enemies under his feet. The last enemy to be destroyed is death.... When all things are subjected to him, then the Son himself

also will be subjected to him who put all things under him. (1 Cor 15:24–28)

The use of *inclusio* in Mark's Gospel ultimately signifies God's cosmic embrace that will bring the universe back to its starting point in the Son of God. At the end of time, Jesus will establish forever the kingdom of God that he preached from the outset of his ministry, saying "The time is fulfilled, and the kingdom of God is at hand; repent and believe in the gospel (Mk 1:15)." Likewise, at the close of his ministry to the Jews, Jesus warned that at the end of the world, "nation will rise against nation, and kingdom against kingdom (Mt 13:8)," but "the gospel must first be preached to all nations (Mt 13:10)."

The Seven Remembrances

Mark's Gospel is a reflection of Peter's eyewitness account of the life of Jesus, and is organized according to Peter's own proclamation of the gospel (Acts 2:14–38, 5:30–32, 10:34–43). This proclamation can be summarized as follows:

1. Jesus fulfilled what was foretold by the prophets of the Old Testament.

2. Jesus was anointed with the Holy Spirit and with supernatural power, and "went about doing good and healing all that were oppressed by the devil (Acts 10:38)."

3. Jesus was delivered to death on the Cross by the set plan of God.

4. By virtue of his resurrection, Jesus was exalted as Lord and Messiah (Christ).

5. The ascension of Jesus to the right hand of God and subsequent outpouring of the Holy Spirit are proof of Jesus' heavenly rule.

6. Salvation is offered to those who repent and believe in the gospel.

7. Jesus will return to judge the living and the dead.

The main ideas of Mark's Gospel can be conveniently summarized by the seven stone memorials left by Joshua to remind future generations of Israel's covenant with God.

The stones of Gilgal (Jos 4:1–3) commemorated the parting of the Jordan and subsequent circumcision of the Israelites, which marked them as children of the Covenant (Gen 17:10–11). The stones foretold the baptism of the Lord Jesus, at which the heavens were torn and the voice of the Father spoke, declaring Jesus his Son (Mk 1:9–11). At Christ's baptism, the Holy Spirit came down and anointed Jesus so that he worked mighty deeds, recalling the miraculous power of God manifested in the parting of the waters.

The stones of Achor commemorated the stoning of Achan, who violated the ban of God and prevented the

Israelites from winning their first battle at Ai (Jos 7:1–26). These stones anticipated Christ's war against sin and his message to repent and believe in the gospel (Mk 1:14–15).

The stones of Ai commemorated the defeat of the king of Ai, who was hung upon a tree (Jos 8:1–29). They represent Christ's victory over sin through the Cross, guaranteed by divine providence (Mk 14:1–15:39).

The altar of unhewn stones at Mount Ebal commemorated the Law of Moses and its blessings and curses (Jos 8:30–35). The altar prefigured the Transfiguration, at which Christ foretold his passion and death that satisfied the curse of the Law, as well as his resurrection that brought to fruition the blessings of eternal life (Mk 9:2–13).

The stones that covered the cave of Makkedah celebrated the victory of the Israelites over the five Amorite kings, who were taken from the cave and hung upon five trees (Jos 10:1–28). They were the fifth of Joshua's memorials, and foreshadowed Christ's victory over death through his resurrection. This victory was symbolized by the stone that was rolled over Christ's tomb, then unrolled by an angel on the third day after Jesus was nailed to the Cross (Mk 15:46–16:6).

The large stone altar near the Jordan commemorated the successful return of the tribes of Reuben, Gad, and Manasseh to their homes on the eastern side of the river, after having helped their fellow Israelites win their territory on the western side (Jos 22:1–34). In building the altar, which they named "Witness," they foreshadowed Christ's ascension whereby he returned to heaven after having conquered man's greatest enemies, sin and death. The immense wealth that the eastern tribes took home with them anticipated the outpouring of the gifts of the Holy Spirit that witness to Jesus' heavenly rule at the right hand of God (Mk 16:14–20).

Finally, the witness stone at Shechem reminded the Israelites of their pledge to serve God, and of Joshua's warning of the judgment that would befall them if they were unfaithful to God's covenant (Jos 23:1–24:29). Joshua died soon after setting up the witness stone, his final memorial pointing to the Last Judgment, when Christ will return to judge the living and the dead (Mk 13:1–36).

The seven stone memorials of Joshua, though no longer visible, remain enshrined in the Gospel of Mark, delineating the boundaries of the spiritual territory conquered by Jesus Christ, the Son of God. He is the true Stone to which the Scriptures bear witness:

> Come to him, to that living stone, rejected by men but in God's sight chosen and precious. . . . For it stands in scripture: "Behold, I am laying in Zion a stone, a cornerstone chosen and precious, and he who believes in him will not be put to shame." (1 Pet 2:4–6)

5

The New Temple:
The Gospel of Luke

The Ox and the Man

Luke, Mark, and Matthew are referred to as the Synoptic Gospels, because they describe the life of Christ with a "similar eye." The fact that they share many of the same details has led modern scholars to conclude that Mark was a common source for Matthew and Luke, in addition to a hypothetical document referred to as "Q" for the German word *Quelle* (Source). However, the Synoptic Gospels are also marked by important differences. Luke, in particular, gives us a picture of the Incarnation that is, among all the gospels, the most complete and universal in appeal. His genealogy of Christ, in contrast to that of Matthew, traces Jesus' physical ancestry all the way back to the dawn of human history, to demonstrate that he is "the son of Adam, the son of God (Lk 3:38)."

Without Luke's Gospel, we would not know much about the early life of Christ, from his birth in Bethlehem to his progress as an adolescent boy becoming a full Son of the Law (*Bar Mitzvah* in Aramaic). It is largely through Luke that we come to know Jesus' mother, Mary, and his inclusive attitude toward women, who made up a significant portion of his followers (Lk 8:2–3). Jesus' visit to the home of Martha and Mary (Lk 10:38–42) is in fact one of Luke's most beloved stories. Luke also pays close attention to the spiritual order, including Jesus' prayer life, the action of the Holy Spirit preceding Pentecost (e.g., Lk 1:35–80), and liturgical worship in the Temple.

The Second Temple, the successor to the original Temple of Solomon, was built by the Jews after the Babylonian Exile and later refurbished by Herod the Great. The Temple was the summit and splendor of Jerusalem, its golden roof visible to pilgrims for miles before they entered the city. Luke's Gospel is largely organized around visits to the Temple in Jerusalem, from the very first chapter where we see Zechariah, the father of John the Baptist, performing his priestly duties at the altar, to the end of the Gospel, when the disciples return to the Temple after witnessing Jesus' ascension into heaven.

Unfortunately, the Temple was obliterated by the Romans during the Jewish Revolt of 70 AD, as Jesus warned before his death, saying "there shall not be left here one stone upon another that will not be thrown down (Lk 21:6)." Only the Western Wall remains to remind us of the pride and glory of the ancient Jews, and of the tragedy that befell them and their quest to re-establish the kingdom of Solomon. To the Christian, however, there stands an everlasting temple in Jesus Christ, the stone the builders rejected that had become the cornerstone (Ps 118:22).

Both the ox and the man epitomize St. Luke. The ox was the animal that gave its blood in perpetual sacrifice at the temple altar. But only the blood of the perfect and guiltless Man could attract divine mercy sufficiently to open the gates of heaven. The Gospel of Luke points to Jesus Christ as the New Temple, the Holy Ox, and the Son of Man, who would inherit an everlasting kingdom (Dan 7:13–14; Lk 1:31–33), unlike the transient kingdoms of David and Solomon, and of their successors among the Jews.

The Historian

Luke was a Greek-speaking physician and very likely one of the earliest native Syrian Christians at Antioch (Acts 11:19–26). According to a tradition dating back to the second century, he spent his last years in Greece, where he wrote his Gospel in a refined style befitting an audience of educated Gentiles. In a prologue patterned after the prefaces of famous Greek histories such as those by Herodotus and Thucydides, Luke dedicated his gospel to a high Roman official named Theophilus (Lk 1:3), assuring him that his sources were drawn from "eyewitnesses and ministers of the word (Lk 1:2)."

As a careful historian, Luke took pains to situate the events of the gospel amid the milestones of Roman politics. For example, in recalling the circumstances of Jesus' birth, he mentioned the census decreed by Caesar Augustus and conducted during the term of Quirinius, the governor of Syria (Lk 2:1–2). Luke also cited the concurrent offices of secular and religious leaders in dating the ministry of John the Baptist (Lk 3:1–2).

Luke was not only steeped in classical learning, but as a convert to Judaism was also well versed in Scripture. In deference to his non-Jewish readers, he did not make as many overt references to the fulfillment of Old Testament prophecy as did Matthew. Nevertheless, beneath the Gentile surface of Luke's Gospel lies a web of interconnections between the history of the Jews and the life of Christ, involving particularly the major storylines of the books of Samuel, Kings, and Chronicles. An example of St. Luke's subtle references to the Historical Books of the Bible may be seen in the following cryptic remark:

> Blessed are the eyes which see what you see! For I tell you that many *prophets and kings* desired to see what you see, and did not see it, and to hear what you hear and did not hear it. (Lk 10:23–24)

By contrast, the corresponding verse in Matthew's gospel (Mt 13:17) substitutes "righteous men" for "kings," reflecting Matthew's preoccupation with the Law of Moses as compared to Luke's focus on the old kingdoms of Israel and Judah.

Luke shows that the life, death, and resurrection of Jesus are the true meaning behind the rise and fall of the kingdom of David and Solomon, the exile of the Jews to Babylon, and their return to Jerusalem to rebuild the

Temple. Luke's view of history, however, goes beyond the fulfillment of Jewish aspirations to the universal kingdom of God that includes people from all nations. His vision is that of the prophet Daniel, who saw

> One like a son of man, and he came to the Ancient of Days and was presented before him. And to him was given dominion and glory and kingdom, that all peoples, nations, and languages should serve him; his dominion is an everlasting dominion, which shall not pass away, and his kingdom one that shall not be destroyed. (Dan 7:13–14)

Side by Side

Among Luke's contemporaries was the Greco-Roman historian, Plutarch, who around 100 AD wrote a famous collection of biographies known as *The Parallel Lives*. As the name of his book suggests, Plutarch presented his classic biographies in pairs (diptychs), alternating between Greek and Roman heroes to draw moral lessons from similarities of character. For example, he paired Alexander the Great with Julius Caesar to compare and contrast the ambitions that led to their careers of conquest.

Luke used the same technique in interspersing various diptychs throughout his Gospel. These diptychs involve pairs of individuals who either lived at the time of Jesus or were drawn from the Historical Books of the Old Testament. The diptych is a pattern especially befitting the

Incarnation, in which the human and divine natures are combined in the person of Jesus Christ, "the son of Adam, the son of God (Lk 3:38)."

John and Jesus

The first and most obvious of Luke's diptychs occurs at the outset of the Gospel, in the nativity stories of John the Baptist and Jesus. These stories are not only full of explicit parallels, beginning with the twin annunciations by the angel Gabriel, but also refer implicitly to the Old Testament pair of Samuel and David. John's prophetic career is clearly similar to that of Samuel, who anointed David king over Israel, just as John baptized Jesus to inaugurate the latter's ministry as the long-awaited Messiah.

Both Samuel and John were Nazirites (males specially consecrated according to the prescriptions of Num 6:1–8), who were conceived by barren women on the presentation of a sacrifice to God (1 Sam 1:1–20; Lk 1:9–15). Jesus' conception was even more unusual in that his mother Mary was a virgin overshadowed by the Holy Spirit. John was in turn filled with the Holy Spirit when he heard Mary's voice while still within the womb of his mother, Elizabeth. His leaping at the voice of Mary recalled King David's joyful dancing before the Ark of the Covenant when the Ark was permanently transferred to Jerusalem (2 Sam 6:1–19).

Mary and Zechariah

John and Jesus, Mary and Elizabeth, and Mary and Zechariah are three pairs of characters explicitly described in
the nativity stories of St. Luke. The last of these diptychs
is enshrined in the Liturgy of the Hours (also known as
the Divine Office), which for centuries has served as the
Church's public prayer throughout the entire day. Zechariah's *Benedictus* (Lk 1:67–79) and Mary's *Magnificat* (Lk
1:46–55) are the hymns chanted or spoken during Morn-
ing and Evening Hours, and are prime examples of the
emphasis on prayer found in Gospel of Luke. The *Magnificat* is based on Hanna's hymn of gratitude in conceiving
the prophet Samuel (1 Sam 2:1–10), while the *Benedictus*
evokes King David's song of thanksgiving at the arrival of
the Ark in Jerusalem (1 Ch 16:7–36).

Bethlehem and Jerusalem

Luke's Christmas story is framed by two cities, Bethlehem and Jerusalem, which were the birthplaces of the
famous kings, David and Solomon (Ruth 1:1, 4:21; 1 Ch
3:5). The name Bethlehem means "House of Bread," while
Jerusalem means "City of Peace," corresponding to
Solomon's name, "The Peaceful One." Bethlehem and
Jerusalem are reminders of the great messianic prophecies of Micah and Ezekiel:

> But you, O Bethlehem Ephrathah . . . from you
> shall come forth for me one who is to be ruler in

Israel. . . . And he shall stand and feed his flock on the strength of the LORD . . . and this shall be peace. (Mic 5:1–5)

I will set over them one shepherd, my servant David, and he shall feed them. . . . I will make with them a covenant of peace. (Ezk 34:23–25)

God's pledges to feed his people and to give them rest are reinforced by Luke's image of the infant Jesus sleeping in a manger or feeding trough. Later, during his public ministry Jesus would say, "I am the bread of life, he who comes to me shall not hunger (John 6:35)," and, "Peace I leave with you; my peace I give to you (John 14:27)."

Christ also called himself "the good shepherd (John 10:11)." St. Luke tells us that, on the night of Jesus' birth in Bethlehem, angels appeared to lowly shepherds, directing them to the manger where Jesus lay, and singing "Glory to God in the highest, and on earth peace among men (Lk 2:14)."

Simeon and Anna

David and Solomon had each played a major role in preparing the First Temple in Jerusalem. It was David who conceived the idea of building the Temple, drew its original plan, ordained its liturgy, organized its priests, and gathered together its materials (1 Ch 23:1–6, 24:1–19, 28:1–29:9). But because David had shed too much blood in warfare, he left it to his son Solomon, the peaceful one, to build and furnish the Temple (1 Ch 28:3). It was Solomon who brought the Ark of the Covenant into the Temple, praying:

> And now arise, O LORD God, and go to your resting place, you and the ark of your might. Let your priests, O LORD God, be clothed with your salvation, and let your saints rejoice in your goodness. (2 Ch 6:41, Ps 132:8–9)

Forty days after Jesus' birth, his parents took him to the Temple to present him to God and to ritually purify his mother according to the demands of the Law (Lev 12:1–8, Lk 2:22–24). As they went about the Temple, they were recognized by two people, Simeon and Anna, who rejoiced upon seeing them (Lk 2:25–38). Simeon's Canticle (Lk 2:29–35), enshrined in the Liturgy of the Hours as the *Nunc Dimittis*, resembles Psalm 132 and Solomon's invocation during the procession of the Ark into the Temple.

Simeon and the elderly widow Anna, like the shepherds to whom angels announced the birth of Jesus, were among the lowly whom God greatly favored. They were like the two young pigeons that Jesus' parents offered as a sacrifice to God at the Temple, an offering reserved for the poor who could not afford a lamb for the holocaust. Luke's Gospel is, among other things, the Gospel of the poor, whom Christ uplifts so that they are seated with princes in the kingdom of God (Lk 1:52).

Elijah and Elisha

The beginning of Jesus' public life in Galilee, as told by Luke, recalls the ministries of the prophets Elijah and Elisha, which are recorded in the books of Kings. Elijah and Elisha were rejected by the people of Israel, but found welcoming hearts among the Gentiles, particularly the Sidonian woman of Zarepath (1 Ki 17:8–24) and Naaman, the Syrian general (2 Ki 5:1–27). Likewise, Jesus was rejected by his own kinfolk at Nazareth (Lk 4:25–39). Because of this, he compared himself to Elijah and Elisha saying, "no prophet is acceptable in his own country (Lk 4:24)."

Elisha had inherited a double portion of the spirit of Elijah, his mentor (2 Ki 2:9). Jesus surpassed them both in the force of his miracles. Whereas Elijah had shut the skies so that no rain fell upon Israel for three and a half years (1 Ki 17:1; Lk 4:25), Jesus calmed a violent storm on the Sea of Galilee in an instant (Lk 8:22–25). Likewise, Jesus multiplied five loaves and two fish to feed a crowd of five thousand (Lk 9:10–17), while Elisha had multiplied twenty loaves of barley and a few ears of grain to feed a mere hundred (2 Ki 4:42–44). Christ's power was such that Herod Antipas, who had John the Baptist beheaded, feared that Jesus was Elijah or else John raised from the dead (Lk 9:7–9), for John himself was reputed to possess the spirit of Elijah (Lk 1:17).

The Widow and the Leper

Jesus inaugurated his Galilean ministry at the synagogue in Nazareth by reading aloud the scroll of Isaiah (Is 61:1–2):

> The Spirit of the LORD is upon me, because he has anointed me to preach good news to the poor. He has sent me to proclaim release to the captives and recovering of sight to the blind, to set at liberty those who are oppressed, to proclaim the acceptable year of the LORD. (Lk 4:18–19)

The poor to whom Christ preached the good news were much like the Gentile characters he alluded to at the synagogue in Nazareth (Lk 4:25–27). The Sidonian woman whom Elijah visited at Zarepath, and Naaman the Syrian, who sought out the prophet Elisha, were typical of those regarded with disdain or condescension by the Israelites, not merely because they were Gentiles, but because one was a poor widow and the other a leper.

Some of the miracles Jesus performed in Galilee recalled those performed by Elijah and Elisha. Elijah had restored to life the widow's dead son, a feat which Jesus duplicated by raising the son of the widow of Nain (Lk 7:11–17). Christ also repeated the miracle of Elisha, who healed the Syrian general of leprosy. Jesus did this by curing a leper before withdrawing to the wilderness (Lk 5:12–16), and later by healing the slave of a Roman centurion at Capernaum (Lk 7:1–10).

Jesus ministered to the lowly and outcast of Jewish society, restoring them to physical and spiritual health. Their liberation from natural and supernatural oppression fulfilled the true meaning of the Jubilee decreed by Moses, that is, the "acceptable year (Lk 4:19)" in which all debts were forgiven, slaves set free, and property restored to their original owners (Lev 25:8–55; De 15:1–18).

Poor and Rich

Naaman the leper and the widow of Zarepath are examples of the *anawim*, that is, the poor who depend only on God for their sustenance and survival. The faces of the *anawim* were typically those of the widow, the orphan, and the alien. Luke's rendering of the Beatitudes (Lk 6:20–26) refers to the *anawim* as the poor, the hungry, the weeping, and the rejected. They are blessed by God, as opposed to the rich, the sated, the laughing, and the favored, who are condemned for overlooking the needs of the poor, just as the rich man ignored Lazarus in Jesus' famous parable (Lk 16:19–31).

Whereas in Matthew's Gospel Jesus proclaimed the Beatitudes on a mountain (Mt 5:1–12), Luke describes a separate event in which Jesus came down from the hills to "a level place (Lk 6:17)." The plain on which Christ delivered his sermon is a fitting reminder that the Son of God descended to earth as the Son of Man to deliver the *anawim* from the proud and the mighty who oppress them. God had once promised the king of Israel, "Because the Syrians have said, 'The LORD is a god of the hills but he is not a god of the valleys,' therefore I will give all this great multitude into your hand, and you shall know that I am the LORD (1 Ki 20:28)." Jesus likewise fulfills Isaiah's prophecy that "every valley shall be lifted up, and every mountain and hill be made low; the uneven ground shall become level, and the rough places a plain (Is 40:4)."

Samaria and Jerusalem

After Jesus' peak experience on Mount Tabor, where he spoke with the prophet Elijah as well as with Moses the lawgiver (Lk 9:28–36), "he set his face to go to Jerusalem (Lk 9:51)." This set the stage for Luke's "travelogue" documenting Jesus' journey from Galilee to the place of his ultimate sacrifice.

To go from Galilee to Jerusalem, Christ and his disciples had to pass through the region of Samaria. Samaria had inherited its name from the old city that had once served as the capital of the northern kingdom of Israel, which split from the southern kingdom of Judah in a rebellion against Solomon's successor, Rehoboam (1 Ki 12:1–24). Centuries later, the northern kingdom fell to the Assyrians, who deported the Israelites and brought in foreigners to replace them (2 Ki 17:22–34). The foreigners were detested by the Jews for their bastardized religion that combined elements of Judaism with pagan practices. The Samaritans of Jesus' day were descended from these enemies of the Jews.

> And he sent messengers ahead of him, who went and entered a village of the Samaritans, to make ready for him; but the people would not receive him, because his face was set toward Jerusalem. And when his disciples James and John saw it, they said, "Lord, do you want us to bid fire come down from heaven and consume them?" But he turned and rebuked them. And they went on to another village. (Lk 9:52–56)

Although the prophet Elijah had once called down fire from heaven against the hundred soldiers sent to arrest him (2 Ki 1:9–12), Jesus refused to do the same, despite the pleas of James and John, for he bore no prejudice against the Samaritans. In his famous parable of the good Samaritan (Lk 10:25–37), he even used one as an example of true charity in contrast to a Jewish priest and a Levite. Nevertheless, Jesus was not a pacifist when it came to fulfilling his mission, for he said:

> I came to cast fire upon the earth; and would that it were already kindled! I have a baptism to be baptized with; and how I am constrained until it is accomplished! Do you think I have come to give peace on earth? No, I tell you, but rather division. (Lk 12:49–51)

The division which ended the kingdom of Solomon would now be applied more generally to the human race. Henceforth, Jesus would divide humanity between the kingdom of the world ruled by Satan and the kingdom of God, over which he would preside.

Judas and Peter / The Two Thieves

Even as Jesus went to the Cross, the judgment of God was already dividing the wheat of his kingdom from the chaff. At the Last Supper, Jesus said to St. Peter, "Simon, Simon, behold, Satan demanded to have you, that he might sift you like wheat (Lk 22:31)." Simon Peter would fail the test of that night by denying Christ three times before the cock crowed (Lk 22:34, 55–60), yet the grace of God would save him (Lk 22:32). The same could not be said for Judas, who, like Peter was one of the twelve chosen by Jesus to be his companions in ministry. Of him Christ said, "For the Son of man goes as it has been determined, but woe to that man by whom he is betrayed (Lk 22:22)."

The same division of souls was at work as Jesus drew his last breath. Of the two thieves who were crucified alongside him, one unrepentantly mocked him, while the other docilely accepted the justice of God (Lk 23:39–43). Christ turned to the latter and said to him, "Truly, I say to you, today you will be with me in Paradise (Lk 23:44)."

When Elijah bested the false prophets of Baal at the test on Mount Carmel (1 Ki 18:17–40), he said to Ahab, the evil king of Israel, "Go up, eat and drink, for there is a sound of the rushing of rain (1 Ki 18:41)." But Ahab did not mount his chariot until the rain fell. After the rainstorm, Elijah fled from Ahab to Mount Horeb (Sinai), where the Lord God said to him, "I will leave seven thousand in Israel, all the knees that have not bowed to Baal, and every mouth that has not kissed him (1 Ki 19:18)." The violent storm that overtook Ahab as he went up to eat and drink signifies the sudden judgment of God that will separate his holy remnant from the world.

> As it was in the days of Noah, so will it be in the days of the Son of man. They ate, they drank, they married, they were given in marriage, until the day when Noah entered the ark, and the flood came and destroyed them all. . . . I tell you, in that night there will be two men in bed; one will be taken and the other left. There will be two women grinding together; one will be taken, the other left. (Lk 17:26–35)

The Jews themselves had already experienced the force of God's judgment, when the Babylonians took captive the last heir to David's throne and utterly destroyed Solomon's Temple. They then deported the Jews to Babylon, leaving only the poor of the land to be vinedressers and plowmen (2 Ki 25:1–12; 2 Ch 36:17–21). The Babylonian Exile lasted several decades, until King Cyrus of Persia, who by then had conquered Babylon, gave permission for the Jews to return home (2 Ch 36:22–23).

As he carried his Cross to Golgotha, Jesus warned the women of Jerusalem, "The days are coming when they will say, 'Blessed are the barren, and the wombs that never

bore, and the breasts that never nursed!' Then they will
begin to say to the mountains, 'Fall on us'; and to the hills,
'Cover us!' For if they do this when the wood is green,
what will happen when it is dry (Lk 23:29–31)?" During
the Roman siege of Jerusalem in 70 AD, women were
forced to eat their own children to avoid starvation, and
the Romans cut down so many trees to crucify the rebels,
that Judea became barren and desolate for two thousand
years. Jesus' own suffering and death were an anticipation
of and participation in the Jewish national calamity of 70
AD, as well as a recollection of what had occurred under
Babylon.

The Two Men in White

The time between the resurrection of Jesus and his ascension into heaven is marked by the two-fold appearance of
two men in dazzling white garments, the first occurring
at the end of Luke's Gospel (Lk 24:4), and the second at
the beginning of his sequel in the Book of Acts (Acts
1:10). These books themselves constitute a diptych presenting two portraits of Jesus Christ, the first of his
human incarnation, and the second of his mystical body,
the Church (1 Cor 12:12–27). Through the Church,
Christ is made present to all ages by a continual expansion
of his heavenly reign, from Jerusalem to the ends of the
earth (Lk 24:47).

The Seven Temple Visits

The Gospel of Luke is ultimately about the Way (Acts 9:2) on which every soul journeys in faith to the living temple of God, as Jesus once traveled the road from Galilee to the Temple of Jerusalem. The road to the living temple that is Jesus Christ is marked by seven signposts, represented in Luke's Gospel by seven visits to the Temple.

The first signpost is marked by Zechariah's entrance into the Temple on the day he was selected by lot to offer incense to God (Lk 1:5–23). In prior salvation history, this corresponds to the call of Samuel as he lay in the presence of the Ark of the Covenant in the house of God at Shiloh (1 Sam 3:1–18). In the life of the individual soul, the first signpost represents the call of grace that must precede any action of the human will.

The second signpost is marked by the presentation of the infant Jesus and the purification of his mother Mary in the Temple, recalling David's penitential sacrifice to God and Solomon's erection of the Temple on the threshing floor of Araunah the Jebusite (2 Sam 24:10–25; 2 Ch 3:1). The second signpost represents the illumination and purification of the soul through repentance from sin and faith in the atoning sacrifice of Christ.

The third signpost is marked by the finding of the adolescent Jesus in the Temple (Lk 2:41–51), corresponding to God's gift of wisdom to King Solomon (1 Ki 3:1–14). The third signpost represents the diligent searching and faithful acceptance of the Word of God, by which the believer grows and matures in spirit.

The fourth signpost is marked by the ascent of Christ to the pinnacle of the Temple, as he struggled with temptation by the devil (Lk 4:1–13). This signpost corresponds to the fall of King Solomon (1 Ki 11:1–13) that divided Judah and Israel, and represents the mortification of the lust of the flesh, the lust of the eyes, and the pride of life (1 Jn 2:16).

The fifth signpost is marked by Christ's cleansing of the Temple, recalling the renovation and reform of the Temple by the Jewish kings Joash (2 Ch 24:1–15), Hezekiah (2 Ch 29:1–21), and Josiah (2 Ch 34:1–35:19). The fifth signpost represents the rejection of idolatry and the cultivation of prayer, for Christ said, "My house shall be a house of prayer (Lk 19:46)."

The sixth signpost is marked by Christ's daily teaching in the Temple during the days preceding his Passion (Lk 19:47–21:38). In his teaching, Jesus warned of the coming destruction of Jerusalem in which the Jews would "fall by the edge of the sword, and be led captive among the nations (Lk 21:24)." The sixth signpost corresponds to the Babylonian Exile, and represents separation from the world through the Cross.

Finally, the seventh signpost is marked by the joyful presence of the disciples in the Temple after the ascension of Christ (Lk 24:52–53). This last signpost recalls the return of the Jews to rebuild the Temple after the Exile (2

Ch 36:22–28). It represents the invisible union with the resurrected Christ, the living temple, manifested in the breaking of the bread at the end of the road to Emmaus (Lk 24:28–35).

6

The New Beginning:
The Gospel of John

The Eagle

It does not take long to realize how different is the Gospel of John from those of Matthew, Mark, and Luke. From the outset John strikes a mystical chord, as if he were hovering above the earth like the Spirit brooding over the face of the waters (Gen 1:2). St. Augustine wrote, "St. John the apostle, not undeservedly in respect of his spiritual understanding compared to the eagle, has elevated his preaching higher and far more sublimely than the other three (*Tractates on the Gospel of John* 36.1)." St. John sees everything from the heavenly perspective. It is John who remembers Jesus' saying to the Pharisees, "You are from below, I am from above (John 8:23)." Likewise, it is the Jesus of John's Gospel who insists that to enter the kingdom of God, one must be born from above (John 3:3).

The phrase "from above," in Greek *anothen*, also means "again" or "anew," hence a common expression among Christians with regard to themselves is that they have been "born again." However, being "born anew" refers to much more than one's spiritual rebirth. It means being part of an entirely new order of things, a second creation, as it were. St. Paul teaches, "if any one is in Christ, he is a new creation; the old has passed away, behold the new has come (2 Cor 5:17)." In the Apocalypse, which John wrote on the island of Patmos, Jesus uses the first and last letters of the Greek alphabet to refer to himself as "the Alpha and the Omega, the first and the last, the beginning and the end (Rev 22:13)." If the Apocalypse is about the Omega or end of the first creation, then the Gospel of John is about the Alpha, the beginning of the new.

John opens his Gospel with the phrase, "In the beginning (John 1:1)," reminding us of the first verse in Genesis: "In the beginning God created the heavens and the earth (Gen 1:1)." The passage in Genesis apparently refers to the beginning of time, but in light of John's Gospel it also places all creation in the *Beginning*, that is *IN* the Alpha who is Christ, the Logos or Word of God, for John says:

> In the beginning was the Word, and the Word was with God, and the Word was God. He was in the beginning with God; all things were made through him, and without him was not anything made that was made. In him was life, and the life was the light of men. (John 1:1–4)

In John's eyes, Jesus Christ is the same Word by which the Father spoke creation into existence: "And God *said*, 'Let there be light; and there was light (Gen 1:3)."

According to tradition, John wrote his Gospel in Ephesus when he was already ninety years old. By then he was much more than the simple fisherman of Galilee whom Jesus chose as one of his first disciples (Mk 1:19–20). While living in Asia Minor, he must have acquired some familiarity with the philosophical traditions of the Greeks, including Heraclitus' concept of the Logos as a "fire" that was the intelligent basis for all reality, revealing truth beyond human speech and reason (also connotations of *logos*).

The combination of Greek philosophical ideas and the Hebrew experience of a personal God resulted in the great synthesis of John's Gospel, which teaches that the Logos is a person, that he is pre-existent, that the Logos became flesh and dwelt among us in human form, that this human being is God himself. (John's insight may also have been fueled by Aramaic translations of the Torah and Nevi'im known as the Targums, which frequently used the term *Memra*, meaning "the Divine Speech," in reference to God.)

The Creative Wisdom

It was the Jewish mystic and philosopher Philo, who first introduced the Hellenic concept of the Logos to Judaism. As a Platonist, Philo was convinced of the superiority of the spiritual order to physical matter. He believed that souls descended into the material realm and that through intellectual contemplation of Plato's invisible Forms, which he interpreted to be the powers of God and the thoughts of his Mind, our souls may ascend back to heaven.

Philo described the Logos as the Form of Forms by which God shaped creation, as if making an impress or copy. The Logos was thus identical to God's Wisdom described in the Book of Proverbs:

> The LORD created me at the beginning of his work, the first of his acts of old. Ages ago I was set up, before the beginning of the earth.... When he established the heavens I was there ... when he marked out the foundations of the earth, then I was beside him, like a master workman; and I was daily his delight ... rejoicing in his inhabited world and delighting in the sons of men. (Pr 8:22–31)

The Hebrew Scriptures were translated into Greek in Philo's native Alexandria, the cosmopolitan city in Egypt founded by and named after Alexander the Great. The translation had been requested by King Ptolemy II and was known in Latin as the *Septuaginta* because it was allegedly composed by seventy Jewish elders (or seventy-two, according to Philo). As the Septuagint developed, it came to be regarded as the authoritative translation of the Jewish Bible in the common language of the Hellenic world and the later eastern Roman Empire. It was repeatedly quoted in the New Testament as an inspired text, even when it diverged from the Hebrew in its literal meaning (e.g. Ps 40:6 as quoted in Heb 10:5).

Within the Septuagint are several original Greek texts considered among the Wisdom Books and regarded as part of the Old Testament by Catholic and Orthodox Christians, who refer to them as the deutero-canonical books. One of these is the Book of Sirach or Ecclesiasticus, in which Wisdom speaks:

> I came forth *from the mouth of the Most High*, and covered the earth like a mist. *I dwelt in high places*, and my throne was in a pillar of cloud. *Alone I have made* the circuit of the vault of heaven, and have walked in the depths of the abyss. In the waves of the sea, *in the whole earth, and in every people and nation* I have gotten a possession. Among all these I sought a resting place; *I sought in whose territory I might lodge.* Then the Creator of all things gave me a commandment, and the one who created me *assigned a place for my tent.* And he said, '*Make your dwelling* in Jacob, and *in Israel receive your inheritance.*' *From eternity, in the beginning*, he created me, and for eternity I shall not cease to exist. (Sir 24:3–9)

Compare these verses with the Prologue of John's gospel:

> *In the beginning . . . the Word was with God.* . . . He was *in the world*, and *the world was made through him*, yet *the world knew him not.* He came to his own home, and *his own people received him not.* But to all who received him . . . he gave power *to become children of God.* And the Word became flesh

and *dwelt* ["pitched his tent"] *among us.* . . . No one has ever seen God; the *only Son*, who is in the bosom of the Father, he has made him known. (John 1:1–18)

The correspondence between these passages points to Jesus as the eternal Wisdom who assisted in the creation of the world, was sent forth from the mouth of God, and descended to the human race. But Wisdom was rejected, except by God's children who are Wisdom's inheritance. In the tradition of the Jews, Wisdom ascended back to heaven after being rejected by men, as stated in the apocryphal book of Enoch (42). This theme of origin and destination, of descent and ascent, is repeated throughout the Gospel of John.

No one has ascended into heaven but he who descended from heaven, the Son of man. (John 3:13)

The chief priests and Pharisees sent officers to arrest him. Jesus then said, "I shall be with you a little while longer, and then I go to him who sent me; you will seek me and you will not find me; where I am you cannot come." (John 7:32–34)

For the Father himself loves you, because you have loved me and have believed that I came from the Father. . . . I came from the Father and have come into the world; again, I am leaving the world and going to the Father. (John 16:27–28)

These verses from John hint at the sifting of human beings according to their acceptance or rejection of the Son of Man, who is Wisdom descended from heaven. This idea is reinforced by another deutero-canonical book, The Wisdom of Solomon:

> For perverse thoughts separate men from God . . . because wisdom will not enter a deceitful soul, nor dwell in a body enslaved to sin. . . . For they reasoned unsoundly, saying to themselves, . . ."Let us lie in wait for the righteous man, because he is inconvenient to us and opposes our actions. . . . He professes to have knowledge of God, and calls himself a child of the Lord. . . . We are considered by him as something base . . . he calls the last end of the righteous happy, and boasts that God is his father. . . . Let us see if his words are true . . . for if the righteous man is God's son, he will help him. . . . Let us test him with insult and torture. . . . Let us condemn him to a shameful death, for according to what he says, he will be protected. (Wis 1:3–4, 2:1, 12–20)

Wisdom is ultimately vindicated by Jesus' obedience to the Father.

> Christ Jesus . . . though he was in the form of God, did not count equality with God a thing to be grasped, but emptied himself, taking the form of a servant. . . . And being found in human form

he humbled himself unto death, even death on a cross. Therefore God highly exalted him and bestowed on him the name which is above every name, that at the name of Jesus every knee should bow . . . and every tongue confess that Jesus Christ is Lord. (Phil 2:5–11)

Big Bang

As we have seen, the Gospel of John mirrors Genesis and the books of the Old Testament that speak of Wisdom and its role in creation. Today, it is anathema to seek the truth regarding the origin of the physical world in the words of Scripture. But if the author of Scripture is God, it should not surprise us that his Word is compatible with what human science at its best reveals (as increasingly realized by respected scientists such as the physicist, Gerald Schroeder of the Weizmann Institute, and the biologist, Andrew Parker of Oxford University).

According to the latest cosmological theory, the universe began as a minute and intensely hot blob of primordial matter/energy, held together by a unity of the four known forces, gravity, electromagnetism, and the strong and weak nuclear forces. As the four forces separated from each other, this dark and formless mass that sprang out of the void from the infinite depths of God (Gen 1:1) suddenly stretched in a rapid inflation. As the new universe expanded and cooled, the "waters" of the first elements began to form, in accord with Genesis' description of those first moments, when "the Spirit of God was moving over the face of the waters (Gen 1:2)." Only later did a burst of radiation occur in which the light separated from the darkness (Gen 1:3).

Once the universe had cooled enough for stars to form, their nuclear furnaces cooked the heavier elements, which gravity then separated from the lighter ones. Thus was born the "firmament" of the heavens that separated the waters below from the waters above (Gen 1:6–7). These waters, after various galactic combinations and recombinations, would eventually gather in one particular place to form the earth, which very early in its existence brought forth life, even under the most hostile conditions (Gen 1:9–12). The earth's eventual capture of the moon, the tidal friction of the oceans, and the moon's progressive recession from the earth, led over eons of time to the current rate of diurnal rotation by which the greater light is distinguished from the lesser light (Gen 1:14–15).

As the regular rhythms of time were established on earth, life would adapt to these rhythms in series of ever increasing complexity, beginning in the oceans, then on the edges of the continents and in the air, bringing forth the large reptiles (Hebrew: *taninim gedolim*, Gen 1:21) and the first winged creatures, and progressively over the land surface of the world, until humans eventually made their appearance (Gen 1:20–28).

All of this took place in six eras of alternating darkness and light, starting with the void and the appearance of the first light, through the formation of the first stars after the fading of the initial burst of cosmic radiation, through the cycle of stellar death and life, the separation of the greater light of the sun from the lesser light of the moon and the stars, the emergence of life in the darkest recesses of the oceans to its appearance in the lighted heavens, until finally the light of reason emerged in man from the dim intelligence of his animal precursors.

The Logos, the Divine Wisdom by whom God made the world at which we rightly gaze in awe and wonder, has a superior plan for our spirits, souls, and eventually our bodies. The new creation has its own primordial elements, of which the Gospel of John speaks repeatedly in paratactic style, often in pairs just as hydrogen and oxygen form water. The words corresponding to these elements are the seed of the new life sown by the Eternal Word (the seminal Logos or *logos spermatikos* of the Stoics).

Water and Spirit

Jesus once traveled by night to visit Nicodemus, his secret admirer in the Sanhedrin, the supreme council of the Jews. He said to his host, "Unless one is born of water and the Spirit, he cannot enter the kingdom of God (John 3:5)." Nicodemus, a scholar of the Law, answered, "How can this be? (John 3:9)." Jesus replied, "Are you a teacher of Israel, and yet you do not understand this? . . . If I had told you earthly things and you do not believe, how can you believe if I tell you heavenly things? (John 3:10–12)."

Nicodemus was likely fluent in both Hebrew and Greek. In these languages of the Old Testament, the word for "spirit" is equivalent to the words for "wind" and "breath." Nicodemus should have recognized that the earthly things Jesus was referring to were described in the first few verses of Genesis, where it says "the Spirit of God was moving over the face of the waters (Gen 1:2)." He should have remembered that God created Adam by breathing his soul into clay watered by a mist (Gen 2:5–7), a process which according to St. Augustine may have occurred in stages (*The Literal Meaning of Genesis* 6.1, 6.14). Yet again, Nicodemus ought to have recalled that God renewed the world at the time of Noah by making a wind sweep away the waters of the Flood (Gen 8:1).

The earthly beginning described in Genesis has its heavenly counterpart within the soul. The movement of God's Spirit in the depths of the heart conceives the grain of faith in place of the void of unbelief. This kernel of the new creation, even smaller than a mustard seed (Mt 17:20), is opened by the water and spirit of Baptism, from which expands the new life of Christ.

Darkness and Light

There is a war at the heart of the gospel, for which reason God calls himself "the Lord of hosts (Is 6:3)." At the dawn of creation, God made not only the material universe, but also the hosts or armies of angelic spirits who either rebelled against the Word or remained faithful to him.

Since then, the God of the armies of heaven has been at war against the forces of darkness because of their rejection of the Son.

> Why do the nations conspire and the people plot
> in vain?
> The kings of the earth set themselves, and the
> rulers take counsel together,
> > against the LORD and his anointed saying,
> 'Let us burst their bonds asunder and cast their
> cords from us. . . .'"
> I will tell of the decree of the LORD: He said to
> me,
> "You are my son, today I have begotten you.
> Ask of me, and I will make the nations your heritage. . . .
> You shall break them with a rod of iron,
> > and dash them in pieces like a potter's
> > vessel." (Ps 2:1–9)

For the eternal God, every day is "today." Every day, the Son of God is begotten by the Father as "the sun of righteousness (Mal 4:2)," just as the light was born on the first day of creation. Every day, the darkness rages against the light of the Son. But, "The light shines in the darkness, and the darkness has not overcome it (John 1:5)."

The believer in Christ shares Jesus' victory over darkness in his daily combat with the powers of evil. "For we are not contending against flesh and blood, but against the principalities, against the powers, against the world rulers of the present darkness, the hosts of wickedness in the heavenly places (Eph 6:12)."

Blood and Water

The victory over evil was won principally on the Cross, when blood and water poured out from Jesus' side pierced by a lance (John 19:34). The Cross is spiritually equivalent to the firmament of the second day of creation, which separated the waters below from the waters above (Gen 1:6–7). Jesus' death on the Cross separates those who will inherit the new earth that is from above from the world that is from below. Once the kingdom of the world is overthrown, the citizens of the heavenly Jerusalem will enjoy the Marriage Feast of the Lamb (Rev 19:9) who says, "Behold, I make all things new (Rev 21:5)."

The hour of consummation upon the Cross was anticipated by the Wedding at Cana (John 2:1–11). Towards the end of the feast, when the bride and groom had run out of wine to serve their guests, Jesus turned water into wine at the request of his mother, Mary. He had earlier said to her, "My hour has not yet come (John 2:4)."

Somewhat later, as Jesus was passing through the Samaritan city of Sychar at noon (John 4:4–67), the same hour at which he would be crucified (John 19:14), Jesus encountered a woman at the well of Jacob. He then offered the Samaritan woman "living water (John 4:10)," as Jacob had once offered well water to his bride Rachel at high noon (Gen 29:1–12). Jesus said, "Whoever drinks of the water that I shall give him will never thirst; [it] will become in him a spring of water welling up to eternal life (John 4:13–14)."

Finally, at the Last Supper, Jesus turned the wine of the Passover celebration into the nuptial blood of the New Covenant. By this blood, and by the water of the Spirit, the waters of the first creation will be transformed at the last hour into the wine of the new heavens and the new earth.

The Vine and the Branches

On the third day of the first creation, God made the dry land appear, saying "Let the earth put forth vegetation, plants yielding seed . . . and trees bearing fruit in which is their seed (Gen 1:11)." Jesus' resurrection on the third day marked the first appearance of the true promised land in which there will be no death, but only life to the full. When his friend Lazarus died, Jesus reassured his sister Martha, "I am the resurrection and the life; he who believes in me, though he die, yet shall he live (John 11:25)."

There is a spiritual reproduction by which the life of the new creation propagates. Jesus said to his disciples, "I am the vine, you are the branches. He who abides in me, and I in him . . . bears much fruit, for apart from me you can do nothing (John 15:5)." Just as God made the world through, with, and in the Logos (John 1:1–3), the life of the new creation is passed down the generations through, with, and in Christ the Vine.

Night and Day

On the fourth day of the first creation, God returned his gaze to the heavenly firmament and separated the greater light from the lesser light, so that these would serve as markers of the signs and seasons (Gen 1:14–19). The new creation likewise requires both greater and lesser lights to mark its progression from seed to full flower. The greater light is Jesus, the Light who ascended to heaven, while the lesser light is the Church, which shines forth in the darkness of Jesus' absence until the dawn of his return.

Jesus said to the Jews, "I am the light of the world; he who follows me will not walk in darkness, but will have the light of life (John 8:12)." Before healing a man who was blind from birth, he said: "We must work the works of him who sent me while it is day; night comes, when no man can work. As long as I am in the world, I am the light of the world (John 9:4–5)." Later, Jesus' disciples cautioned him about returning to Judea, where the Jews were prepared to stone him. He replied:

> Are there not twelve hours in the day? If any one walks in the day, he does not stumble, because he sees the light of this world. But if any one walks in the night, he stumbles, because the light is not in him. (John 11:9–10)

It was only at the Last Supper, when Judas left Jesus to betray him that St. John finally acknowledged that "it was night (John 13:30)."

The World and its Ruler

On the fifth day of the first creation, God made the creatures of the sea and sky, including "the great sea monsters (Greek: *ta kiti ta megala*, Gen 1:21)," as a prelude to the work of the sixth day, when he would create the land animals and finally man.

In Scripture, the turbulent waters of the ocean were used as a symbol for the enemies of the righteous, as in the Psalms:

> He reached from on high, he took me, he drew me out of many waters. He delivered me from my strong enemy and from those who hated me. (Ps 18:16–17)

> You divided the sea by your might, you broke the heads of the dragons on the waters. (Ps 74:13)

The spiritual enemies of man are collectively referred to in John's gospel as the "world" or "cosmos," whose ruler is "the prince of the power of the air, the spirit that is now at work in the sons of disobedience (Eph 2:2)." In this sense, the word "cosmos" refers to a malicious adornment similar to the cosmetics of a harlot, a vain spiritual order that opposes the will of God. "He was in the world . . . but the world did not know him (John 1:10)." In his first epistle, St. John warns us: "Do not love the world or the things in the world. If any one loves the world, love for the Father is not in him (1 Jn 2:15)."

When Jesus prayed to the Father during the Last Supper, he refused to pray for the world (John 17:9), and instead blessed those whom the Father had given him:

> I have given them your word; and the world has hated them because they are not of the world, even as I am not of the world. I do not pray that you should take them out of the world, but that you should keep them from the evil one. They are not of the world, even as I am not of the world. (John 17:14–16)

Earlier, in anticipation of his death on the Cross, Jesus had said, "Now is the judgment of this world, now shall the ruler of this world be cast out; and I, when I am lifted up from the earth, will draw all men to myself (John 12:31–32)."

Flesh and Spirit

The creatures that God made on the sixth day of creation were the pinnacle of biological life on earth. But God intended to go even further in creating a masterpiece of the spirit. That masterpiece was man.

What distinguished man from the animals was not only the breath of God that was his spirit, but the divine qualities of grace and truth. Grace is the merciful love of God that elevates man's nature from that of a mere animal to that of God himself, for "God is love (1 Jn 4:8)." Truth, on the other hand, is the enduring substance of God that also makes man like his maker, a rock of fidelity and trustworthiness. "The grass withers, the flower fades; but the word of our God will stand forever (Is 40:8)." Likewise, Jesus said, "Heaven and earth will pass away, but my words will not pass away (Mt 24:35)."

When man first sinned, grace and truth were depleted in him by his disobedience to God, so that man became mere flesh, prone to hatred and the corruption of death. In this way, man lost his power to keep God's commandments. But Jesus came to restore man to his earlier state. "For the law was given through Moses; grace and truth came through Jesus Christ (John 1:17)." Because of this, man is now able to go beyond the Law of Moses and keep the new commandment Jesus gave at the Last Supper: "Love one another; even *as I have loved you* (John 13:34)."

Jesus did more than give a new commandment at the Last Supper; he bequeathed a new food to the human race, just as God had given men food to eat on the day of their creation, saying, "Behold, I have given you every plant yielding seed which is upon the face of all the earth, and every tree with seed in its fruit; you shall have them for food (Gen 1:29–30)."

The food of the new creation is Christ himself, for he said: "I am the bread of life; he who comes to me shall not hunger, and he who believes in me shall never thirst . . . if any one eats of this bread, he will live for ever; and the bread which I will give for the life of the world is my flesh (John 6:35, 51)."

The Bread of Life is the sacrifice offered to God in the Lord's Supper (the equivalent of the Jewish *Todah* or thanksgiving sacrifice). It is not the fallen flesh of Adam, but the flesh of Jesus raised and glorified by the Spirit of God. For Jesus also said, "It is the spirit that gives life, the flesh is of no avail; the words that I have spoken to you are spirit and life (John 6:63)."

The Sheep and the Shepherd

God had made the animals as companions to Adam, who then named them as he willed (Gen 2:18–20). Jesus is likewise the Good Shepherd, who "calls his own sheep by name and leads them out . . . and the sheep follow him, for they know his voice (John 10:3–4)." Jesus protects his sheep, for he says:

> I am the door of the sheep . . . if any one enters by me, he will be saved, and will go in and out to find pasture. The thief comes only to steal and destroy; I came that they may have life, and have it abundantly. I am the good shepherd. The good shepherd lays down his life for the sheep. . . . I know my own and my own know me. (John 10:7–14)

The Woman and the Garden

God placed Adam in the Garden of Eden, in the middle of which stood the Tree of Life and the Tree of the Knowledge of Good and Evil (Gen 2:8–9). He then fashioned Eve from the rib of Adam, and gave her to him as a helper (Gen 2:18, 21–22). Adam called his new helpmate

"Woman, because she was taken out of Man (Gen 2:23)."
But the woman was deceived by the serpent, and gave
Adam the fruit of the knowledge of good and evil, from
which came the sin of the world (Gen 3:1–6).

The Gospel of John is the new Genesis. John presents
Jesus as the new Adam from whose side the Church was
born, and the Cross as the new Tree of Life. At the foot of
this tree stood Mary, the mother of Jesus whom he
addressed as "Woman (John 19:26)." Further John tells
us, "Now in the place where he was crucified there was a
garden, and in the garden a new tomb where no one had
ever been laid (John 19:41)."

It was at the tomb of Jesus that Mary Magdalene first
saw the resurrected Christ, thinking that he was the gar-
dener. Jesus asked her, "Woman, why are you weeping
(John 20:15)?" He then said to her, "I am ascending to my
Father and your Father, to my God and your God (John
20:17)."

Father and Son

Adam and Eve were commanded by God: "Be fruitful and
multiply (Gen 1:28)." But before they could do so, they
fell from grace and were cast out of Eden. The way to the
Tree of Life was then hidden from them (Gen 3:24).
Though Adam was created as "the son of God (Lk 3:38),"
his offspring would no longer be God's children until the
redemption of Christ restored the original truth of creation.

Jesus said, "I am the way, and the truth, and the life; no one comes to the Father, but by me (John 14:6)." When the apostle Philip asked Jesus, "Lord, show us the Father, and we shall be satisfied (John 14:8)," he replied:

> Do you not believe that I am in the Father and the Father is in me? The words that I speak to you I do not speak on my own authority; but the Father who dwells in me does his works. Believe me that I am in the Father and the Father is in me; or else believe me for the sake of the works themselves. (John 14:10–11)

The intimate union between the Father and the Son is illustrated by the miracle Jesus performed on the Sabbath, when he healed a paralytic at the pool by the Sheep Gate (John 5:1–9). Because he had done this on the Sabbath, the seventh day on which God rested from his creation (Gen 2:3), the Jews criticized Jesus. He answered them:

> My Father is working still, and I am working.... The Son can do nothing of his own accord, but only what he sees the Father doing; for whatever he does, that the Son does likewise. For the Father loves the Son, and shows him all that he himself is doing. (John 5:17–20)

In Spirit and Truth

The Jews prided themselves on their stringent observance of the Law of Moses, and of the Sabbath rest in particular.

Jesus did not deny the importance of Jewish belief and practice, for he readily admitted that "salvation is from the Jews (John 4:22)." However, the Jews had forgotten that the true worship of God was not one of mere form, but of spirit and truth, for as Jesus said to the Samaritan woman at the well of Jacob, "God is spirit, and those who worship him must worship in spirit and truth (John 4:24)."

True worship consists of faith in God's word, which is truth itself (John 17:17), and openness to his mercy (grace), which inwardly heals us. Once we have rested in God's mercy and truth, we may participate in the work of the Spirit of truth (John 14:17).

> My food is to do the will of him who sent me, and to accomplish his work.... I tell you, lift up your eyes, and see how the fields are already white for harvest. He who reaps receives wages, and gathers fruit for eternal life, so that sower and reaper may rejoice together. (John 4:34–38)

Jesus promised fullness of joy, "grace upon grace (John 1:16)," to those who are willing to endure the sorrow of spiritual labor (John 16:20–24), so that they may be fruitful and multiply in their sowing and reaping.

> May those who sow in tears reap with shouts of joy! He that goes forth weeping, bearing the seed for sowing, shall come home with shouts of joy, bringing his sheaves with him. (Ps 126:5–6)

The fullness of joy is accompanied by the peace of the true Sabbath, for Jesus said, "Peace I leave with you; my peace I give to you; not as the world gives do I give to you. Let not your hearts be troubled, neither let them be afraid (John 14:27)." And again, "I have said this to you, that in me you may have peace. In the world you have tribulation; but be of good cheer, I have overcome the world (John 16:33)."

The Name and the Glory

On Palm Sunday, there gathered a great crowd in Jerusalem to celebrate the coming Passover. Among the crowd were some Greeks who wished to see Jesus through the good graces of the apostles, Philip and Andrew (John 12:20–22). It was on this occasion, after Jesus had entered Jerusalem to shouts of "Hosanna," that Jesus cried out to God:

> "Father, glorify your name." Then a voice came
> from heaven, "I have glorified it, and I will glorify
> it again (John 12:28–29)."

The word "glory" means "weight" (*kabod*) in Hebrew and "radiance" (*doxa*) in Greek. The weight of the glory of God is so great that it crushes the mountains of human pride, that they may not obscure the radiance of God's glory. The prophet Isaiah wrote:

> Every valley shall be lifted up, and every moun-
> tain and hill be made low; the uneven ground

shall become level, and the rough places a plain.
And the glory of the Lord shall be revealed. (Is
40:4–5)

When Moses asked God to see his glory on Mount
Sinai, the Lord hid him in the cleft of a rock, then passed
by him pronouncing his mysterious name (YHWH).
Afterwards, Moses descended from the mountain with a
face so radiant that it had to be covered with a veil (Ex
34:29–35). To the Israelites, on the other hand, "the
appearance of the glory of the LORD was like a devouring
fire on the top of the mountain (Ex 24:17)."

The name that the Father glorified at Mount Sinai, and
would glorify again in Christ, was the same name spoken
to Moses at the burning bush (Ex 3:13–14). To the Greek
speakers who read the Septuagint, such as those whom
Philip and Andrew introduced to Jesus, that name was
understood metaphysically, and can be rendered "I AM,"
referring to God's eternal being. But in Hebrew, God's
name is more intimate, and is better translated as "I AM
THERE." "For where two or three are gathered in my
name, *there am I* in the midst of them (Mt 18:20)." On the
eve of his death, Jesus prayed to the Father:

Father, I desire that they also, whom you have
given me, may be *with me where I am*, to behold my
glory which you have given me in your love for
me before the foundation of the world. (John
17:24)

The glory given to Jesus communicates the very presence of God, the palpable weight of dense rock, the radiant and consuming fire like that of the burning bush on Mount Sinai, that only the holy can withstand. The wicked will be crushed and devoured by this presence, but the just will find peace and comfort in it. Before Moses asked to see God's glory, God said to him, "My presence will go with you; and I will give you rest (Ex 33:14)."

Jesus claimed the name of God for himself. When asked if he was greater than Abraham, he replied, "If I glorify myself, my glory is nothing; it is my Father who glorifies me. . . . Truly, truly, I say to you, before Abraham was, I AM (John 8:54–58)."

The Seven Signs

The purpose of the Gospel of John is clearly stated by its author, who insists that he was an eyewitness of the events he described. John confesses, "He who saw it has borne witness—his testimony is true, and he knows that he tells the truth—that you also may believe (John 19:35)."

The careful reader will notice that John's account is full of legal references, as if the human race were on trial. Early in the gospel, John the Baptist is called as a witness to testify to Jesus as the Light of God (John 1:6–7, 15, 19–28). Though Jesus did not come to condemn the world but to save it, those who refuse to believe in him are to be judged, because "they loved darkness rather than the light (John 3:19)."

According to John, the Father has commended all judgment to the Son (John 5:23), who states. "I can do nothing on my own authority; as I hear I judge; and my judgment is just, because I seek not my own will but the will of him who sent me (John 5:30)." When Jesus was asked by the scribes and Pharisees to judge a woman caught in adultery, he refused to condemn her, saying "Let him who is without sin among you be the first to throw a stone (John 8:7)." He then turned to the Pharisees, "You judge according to the flesh, I judge no one. Yet even if I do judge, my judgment is true, for it is not I alone that judge, but I and he who sent me (John 8:15–16)."

At the Last Supper, Jesus spoke to the disciples of his return to the Father, and of the coming of the Holy Spirit, whom Jesus referred to as the Paraclete (Greek: *paraklitos*), a legal term denoting an advocate or counselor.

> I tell you the truth: it is to your advantage that I go away, for if I do not go away, the Counselor will not come to you; but if I go, I will send him to you. And when he comes, he will convince the world of sin and of righteousness and of judgment. (John 16:7–8)

As in a court of law, John provides evidence in support of his testimony to Christ. This evidence consists of seven miracles that point to Jesus as the Creator of the world and the bearer of God's name I AM, first revealed to Moses, the author of the Jewish law. John refers to each miracle as a "sign" (Greek: *semeion*), because of its deeper meaning expounded in one of the long discourses unique to John's gospel. These discourses demonstrate that Jesus is the very Wisdom of God. The seven signs are presented here, not in the order that they appear in the Gospel of John, but according to their symbolic references to the seven days of Creation.

The Resurrection

The first of the seven signs occurred on the first day of the week. At the beginning of Jesus' ministry, the Jews had asked him for a sign as proof of his authority to cast out the money-changers from the Temple (an act he would repeat before his death). He replied, "Destroy this temple, and in three days I will raise it up (John 2:19)." The Jews misunderstood this as a reference to the physical Temple.

> But he spoke of the temple of his body. When therefore he was raised from the dead, his disciples remembered that he had said this. (John 2:21–22)

Towards the end of his public ministry, Jesus again visited the Temple on the Feast of the Dedication (*Hanukkah*), commemorating its restoration by the Maccabees after it had been defiled by the Greek tyrant, Antiochus Epiphanes (1 Mac 4:36–59). While standing at Solomon's Portico, Jesus spoke of the sheep who recognized his voice, because they had been given to him by the Father (John 10:22–30). Before this he had said of himself, "I AM the door of the sheep (John 10:7)."

Jesus' resurrection is indeed the door to the new life. His tomb was like the void from which the first creation sprang into existence. Jesus rose just before dawn (John 20:1), for he is the light that marks the first day of the new creation.

Water into Wine

Jesus turned water into wine at the wedding feast at Cana (John 2:1–11), recalling the separation of the waters by the firmament on the second day of Creation. The miracle at Cana anticipated the Last Supper, when Christ said, "I AM the Vine (John 15:5)."

The Raising of Lazarus

The emergence of the land from beneath the waters on the third day of Creation foreshadowed the Resurrection. Christ's resurrection from the dead was preceded by his raising of Lazarus, a sign which affirmed the truth of Jesus' statement, "I AM the resurrection and the life (John 11:25)."

The Healing of the Blind Man

Christ restored the sight of the blind beggar near the Pool of Siloam (John 9), in accordance with his claim, "I AM the light of the world (John 9:5)." Moreover, Christ said: "I came into this world, that those who do not see may see, and that those who see may become blind (John 9:39)." Jesus' healing of the blind beggar and his statement overheard by the Pharisees, who claimed to see (John 9:40–41), correspond to the separation of the greater light from the lesser light on the fourth day of Creation.

The Pool by the Sheep Gate

The pool by the Sheep Gate was known for its miracles attributed to an angel who would stir the waters so that anyone stepping in the pool would be healed (John 5:3–4). The miracles recalled the appearance of life in the waters and in the skies on the fifth day of Creation. The paralytic whom Jesus healed had no one to help him into the pool. Instead of helping him into the pool, Jesus commanded him to take up his pallet and walk (John 5:5–9). The pronouncement, "I AM the Good Shepherd (John 10:11)," reminds us of Jesus' sign at the Sheep Gate.

The Multiplication of the Loaves

Jesus' multiplication of the loaves on the Feast of Passover recalls to the sixth day of Creation, when God gave man and the animals their food. On this occasion Christ said, "I AM the bread of life (John 6:35)."

The Official's Son

After journeying through Samaria, where he had encountered the woman at the well of Jacob, Jesus returned to Cana in Galilee. There he was approached by an official of the city of Capernaum, whose son was at the point of death (John 4:46–54). When the official begged Jesus to heal his son, Jesus replied, "Go; your son will live (John 4:50)."

The official believed Jesus immediately, and while he was yet on his way home, his servants told him that his son had been healed at the very hour that he had trusted Jesus. The sign he was given underscores Christ's message, "I AM the way, the truth, and the life (John 14:6)." It also reminds us of the seventh day of Creation, for the miracle had taken place at the seventh hour (John 4:52).

The miracles and teachings of Jesus are the basis for God's judgment of the world (John 12:44–50), by which he will separate those who by faith recognize the glory of God from the rest who prefer human praise (John 12:43). The supernatural density and brilliance of God's Word will harden the latter's hearts and blind their eyes, as warned by the prophet Isaiah (Is 6), who "saw [God's] glory and spoke of him (John 12:41)."

> Though he had done so many signs before them, yet they did not believe in him; it was that the word spoken by the prophet Isaiah might be fulfilled. . . . "He has blinded their eyes and hardened their heart, lest they should see with their eyes and perceive with their heart, and turn for me to heal them." (John 12:37–40)

The seven signs of John's Gospel reinforce Jesus' claim on our belief. They are the final instance of the Gospel keys, and the appropriate occasion for the reader of this book to ask at last, "Do I believe?"

7

Three Times Two Times Four

Now that we have discovered the keys that unlock the hidden treasures of the Gospels, let us turn to the man at the heart of their message. Remember that the ancient Israelites and Jews used the practice of *gematria* to spiritually decipher words or phrases. It is quite revealing to apply this practice to the greatest name in all of history.

The name Jesus, when written in Greek, has the numerical value 888. The threefold repetition of the number eight is a reminder that, although Jesus is fully human, as a person of the Trinity he shares the divine nature with his Father and the Holy Spirit.

The number eight itself is equal to the sum of the numbers seven and one. Because there are seven days in the Judeo-Christian week corresponding to the seven days of Creation, the sum of seven and one represents a new beginning. The number eight is also twice four, and since four is a symbol of Creation, eight is a symbol for the Second or New Creation.

The Resurrection of Christ occurred on the first day of the week, the eighth day after Jesus' last entry into Jerusalem on Palm Sunday. The Resurrection inaugurated the New Creation, which will ultimately be expressed in the

New Jerusalem at the end of time, when Christ will return to judge the living and the dead.

Because Jesus is God, the acceptance or rejection of his message in the Gospels has eternal consequences for every human being, and for the entire universe as well.

> For the creation waits with eager longing for the revealing of the sons of God . . . because the creation itself will be set free from its bondage to decay and obtain the liberty of the children of God. (Rom 8:19–21)

Little do we know what awaits us on the other side of time, how the Church will live out in full her destiny as the Bride of Christ. St. Paul wrote, "Do you not know that we are to judge angels (1 Cor 6:3)?" For all we know, angels may not be the only creatures we are to judge, or to whom we will minister in love and in the common worship of God.

Whatever fate awaits us in eternity, we can rest assured that the universe is run by a benevolent, all-knowing, and all-powerful God, who draws straight with the crooked lines of sinful human choices. Proof of this lies in the wonderfully coherent and ordered message that is the Bible, as deciphered by the four keys of the Gospels.

The four Gospels of Matthew, Mark, Luke, and John all point to Jesus Christ as the human condensation of the infinite Wisdom and Power of God. He is the divine law-giver, the ultimate conqueror of the enemies of God, the goal and fulfillment of all human history, and the Word through whom all universes, past, present, and future, have been and will be spoken into existence. With all the angels and saints, we will bow down to him in worship at the throne of the living God forever and ever. Amen.

Bibliography

Allen, D. *Philosophy for Understanding Theology*. Atlanta, GA: John Knox Press, 1985.

Aquinas, Thomas. *Catena Aurea: Commentary on the Four Gospels Collected out of the Works of the Fathers*. Albany, NY: Preserving Christian Publications, 1995.

Augustine. *Tractates on the Gospel of John*, 36. The Fathers of the Church. Available at http://www.newadvent.org/fathers/1701036.htm.

———. *The Literal Meaning of Genesis*. Translated by J.H. Taylor. New York: Newman Press, 1982.

———. *Questions on the Heptateuch* 2.73. Cited in *Catechism of the Catholic Church* 129, New York: Doubleday, 1995.

Bacon, B.W. *Studies in Matthew*. London: Constable, 1930.

Barclay, W. *Introduction to John and the Acts of the Apostles*, Philadelphia, PA: The Westminster Press, 1976.

———. *The Gospel of Mark*. Louisville, KY: Westminster John Knox Press, 1995.

———. *The Gospel of Luke*. Louisville, KY: Westminster John Knox Press, 1994.

Brown, R.E. *An Introduction to the New Testament*. New

York: Doubleday, 1997.

―――. *The Death of the Messiah, from Gethsemane to the Grave: A Commentary on the Passion Narratives in the Four Gospels.* New York: Doubleday, 1994.

―――. *The Birth of the Messiah: A Commentary on the Infancy Narratives in the Gospels of Matthew and Luke.* New York: Doubleday, 1977.

Buber, M. *On the Bible: Eighteen Studies.* Edited by N. N. Glatzer. New York: Schocken Books, 1982.

Carson, D. A. "Matthew." In *The Expositor's Bible Commentary.* Edited by F. E. Gaebelein. Vol. 8. Grand Rapids, MI: Zondervan Publishing House, 1984.

Constable, T. L. *Notes on Matthew,* available at: http://www.soniclight.com/constable/notes/pdf/matthew.pdf.

Eusebius. *The History of the Church.* New York: Penguin Books, 1984.

Fenton, J. C. *The Gospel of St. Matthew.* New York: Penguin Books, 1980.

Fuller, R. C., L. Johnston, and C. Kearns. *A New Catholic Commentary on Holy Scripture.* New York: Thomas Nelson Publishers, 1975.

Gray, T. *Mission of the Messiah: On the Gospel of Luke.* Steubenville, OH: Emmaus Road Publishing, 1998.

The Greek New Testament. Edited by K. Aland, M. Black, C. M. Martini, B. M. Metzger, and A. Wikgren. 3rd ed. Stuttgart: United Bible Societies, 1983.

Griffith-Jones, R. *The Four Witnesses.* San Francisco: Harper, 2001.

Guthrie, W. K. C. *History of Greek Philosophy.* Vol. I. Cambridge [etc.]: Cambridge University Press, 1979.

Hahn, S. and C. Mitch. *The Gospel of Mark.* San Francisco: Ignatius Press, 2001.

Holy Bible: Revised Standard Version. 2nd Catholic Edition. San Francisco: Ignatius Press, 2002.

Hunter, C. F. and R. Buck. *Angels on Assignment.* Kingwood, TX: Hunter Books, 1979.

Josephus, Flavius. *The Wars of the Jews.* Vol. 1 *The Works of Flavius Josephus.* Translated by W. Whiston. Grand Rapids, MI: Baker Book House, 1984.

Moeller, H. R. "Wisdom Motifs and John's Gospel." *Bulletin of the Evangelical Theological Society* 6, no. 3 (1963): 92–100.

The NIV Study Bible: New International Version. Edited by K. D. Barker, D. Burdick, J. Stek, W. Wessel, and R. Youngblood. Grand Rapids, MI: Zondervan, 1985.

Olaguer, E. P. *Born from Above: A Commentary on John's Gospel.* Worcester, MA: Ambassador Books, 1998.

_____. *The Old and the New: A Dual Commentary on Genesis and the Gospel of St. Matthew.* Lincoln, NE: Writers Club Press, 2002.

————. *Son of God, Son of Man: On the Gospels of St. Mark and St. Luke*. Xlibris Corporation, 2008.

Parker, A. *The Genesis Enigma: Why the Bible is Scientifically Accurate*. New York: Dutton, 2009.

Rohl, D. *From Eden to Exile: The 5000-Year History of the People of the Bible*, Lebanon, TN: Greenleaf Press, 2002.

Schroeder, G. L. *The Science of God: The Convergence of Scientific and Biblical Wisdom*, New York: The Free Press, 1997.

Septuaginta. Edited by A. Rahlfs. Stuttgart: Deutsche Bibelgesellschaft, 1979.

Tenney, M. C. "The Gospel of John." In *The Expositor's Bible Commentary*. Edited by F. E. Gaebelein. Vol. 8. Grand Rapids, MI: Zondervan Publishing House, 1981.

Ulansey, D. "The Heavenly Veil Torn: Mark's Cosmic Inclusio." *Journal of Biblical Literature* 110(1991): 123–125.

White, L. M. *From Jesus to Christianity*. San Francisco: Harper, 2004.

Wijngaards, J. *Experiencing Jesus*. Notre Dame, IN: Ave Maria Press, 1981.

Witherington, B. *John's Wisdom: A Commentary on the Fourth Gospel*. Louisville, KY: Westminster John Knox Press, 1995.

Appendix:
Abbreviations for Biblical Books

Gen	Genesis
Ex	Exodus
Lev	Leviticus
Num	Numbers
De	Deuteronomy
Jos	Joshua
Ruth	Ruth
1 Sam	First Book of Samuel
2 Sam	Second Book of Samuel
1 Ki	First Book of Kings
2 Ki	Second Book of Kings
1 Ch	First Book of Chronicles
2 Ch	Second Book of Chronicles
1 Mac	First Book of Maccabees
Ps	Psalms
Pr	Proverbs
Wis	Wisdom of Solomon
Sir	Sirach
Is	Isaiah
Jer	Jeremiah
Ezk	Ezekiel
Dan	Daniel
Hos	Hosea
Mic	Micah
Mal	Malachi
Mt	The Gospel of Matthew
Mk	The Gospel of Mark
Lk	The Gospel of Luke

John   The Gospel of John
Acts   Acts of the Apostles
Rom   Romans
1 Cor   First Letter of Paul to the Corinthians
2 Cor   Second Letter of Paul to the Corinthians
Eph   Ephesians
Phil   Philippians
Heb   Hebrews
1 Pet   First Letter of Peter
1 Jn   First Letter of John
Rev   The Revelation to John